0061395

THE COMPLETE POTTER:

HAND-BUILT

CERAMICS

1 Pueblo pottery vase. Decorated with digestive tract and uterus of an animal, from New Mexico, Colarado. This decoration enabled the animals to reproduce and eat in the next world. (Courtesy of the trustees of the British Museum)

THE COMPLETE POTTER:
HAND-BUILT CERAMICS

JANE WALLER

SERIES EDITOR EMMANUEL COOPER

B.T. Batsford Ltd, London

'Technique is a means to an end. It is no end in itself.'
Bernard Leach, *A Potter's Book*, 1940

ISBN 0 7134 6258 2

Typeset by Servis Filmsetting Ltd
and printed in Hong Kong
for the publishers
B.T. Batsford Ltd
4 Fitzhardinge Street
London W1H 0AH

The front cover shows a millefiori bowl by Jane Waller; the small patterns of stained clay were built up inside a mould to form a kaleidoscope of colour. (*Courtesy of Souren Melikian; photo by Steven Woolf*). The back cover shows a raku pinch pot by Jane Waller. (*Photo by Frank Thurston*)

This book is dedicated to those who taught me all I know about ceramics.

CONTENTS

PREFACE

When writing this book, I decided that to give technical advice alone would be to make it like any other craft book. Therefore, I have discussed ways in which the potter can gather inspiration from within as well as around; from contemporary works or from earlier civilizations which involved a strong mythology in their ceramic tradition.

Many of the technical methods are given in the order in which I progressed. Often, what I considered at the time to be my own inventions, I later found had already been done one thousand years earlier! By discoveries made through trial and error, however, a potter can develop a personal style. But he or she must always realize the need to relate decoration to form and to consider the inner and outer space of a piece of work.

I have given the 'advanced' technique for each method so that everything can be learned correctly from the start. Tips are included where there are difficult problems. It is wise not to start work until you have read through a complete method: you need to know that the right equipment is available, the clay prepared, and how much time you will need – some processes require extra time during the making to allow work to firm up.

CHAPTER ONE

Part One: Materials and Techniques

INSPIRATION

Today more than ever before the field is wide open to experiment; all the old rules are open to question, though that is not to say that they will be found invalid; but it does mean that every potter can now make whatever kind of pottery he pleases, and that he alone is responsible.

Dora Billington, *The Technique of Pottery*
1974

CERAMIC HAND-BUILDING TRADITION

Ever since the invention of the potter's wheel, thrown pottery has dominated in the West. It is only during the latter part of this century that there has been a revival of interest in

2 Decorated pre-dynastic pot. Bearing the earliest representation of a ship under sail. From Egypt, Naqada 11 Period, before 3100 BC. (Courtesy of the trustees of the British Museum)

hand-building. Potters began to realize the potential freedom of form that hand-building could give, once they were released from the pressure of making shapes and designs dictated by convention. The historical dominance of wheel-thrown pottery means we must to look either to pre-wheel traditions or to those cultures which never learned or accepted the use of the wheel, such as in Africa or on the American Indian Reserves, to find inspiration for hand-built forms.

All hand-built ceramic forms of today owe their origins to ancient tradition. It was usually the women of those cultures who made and decorated pottery. Designs were therefore based on motifs associated with textile patterns and basket-weaving – both women's occupations traditionally – while forms were based on the need for fireside receptacles. With the invention of the wheel, however, pottery became a mainly male occupation, and so feminine influence inevitably diminished. Desmond Morris wrote in his book on Cypriot Neolithic pottery, *The Art of Ancient Cyprus*, that during the time when the Bronze age gave way to the Iron age:

3 Kamares-style pithos. Decorated with palm trees painted white and red on a dark ground, from Phaistos, Crete. Minoan Old Palace Period 2000–1700 BC (Courtesy of the Heraklion Museum)

The earlier vessels had been made by women in a simple domestic setting, . . . But now, with the introduction of a special 'pottery machine', the males take over and turn what had been a lovingly executed art-form into a mass-production business . . . the geometrically improved shapes lose a great deal of their playful individualism . . . Bands and circles of dark lines are now also made by mechanical means . . . robbing them of a great deal of the human warmth of earlier hand-drawn patterns.

In this book, therefore, the illustrations fall into two categories; ancient pottery from pre-wheel cultures; and contemporary hand-built works that show a versatile and expressive quality helpful to potters today.

CONTENT

All works of art are more beautiful when they suggest something beyond themselves than when they end up being merely what they are
Sōetsu Yanagi, *The Unknown Craftsman.*

As potters are open to the influence of pots from every part of the world, the first step poses several questions:
- What *type* of pot should I make?
- What *form* should I give it?
- How should it be *decorated*?

For most methods it is better to have a strong idea before you start work, because this is bound to be reflected in the pot itself, which will attain a definite presence, a character of its own. (Though for a pinch pot it can be interesting to allow the pot to follow the pinching process.)

In ancient times, while most pottery was created for practical day to day use – cooking, carrying water or storing grains – certain 'special pots' were endowed with strong mythical, religious or ritual values. Some were used as burial receptacles and vessels containing votive offerings to ancestral spirits, and others were decorated with representations of deities.

Ceramics today do not have such an important role to play. With such powerful motives lost we cannot expect to find equal depth of content in our own work, but this should not prevent us from looking back to civilizations which offered a spiritual dimension in their work.

THE MIMBRES TRIBE OF SOUTH WESTERN AMERICAN INDIANS

Pottery was one of the Mimbres main art forms (see page 10), and it embodied a strong mythology. The Mimbres tribe buried their dead beneath the huts they lived in, and when a person died, a delicately-constructed and decorated bowl was placed to cover the face. In the centre of the bowl a small hole was made, presumably to allow the spirit to fly away to join the ancestors. Again, the pots were probably made and decorated by the women, who created them dome-shaped like the universe and peopled them with animals and spirits. These fine works of art were created for only 600 years, between AD 550–1150, but their impact is considerable. A book by J.J. Brody has recently been published called *Mimbres Pottery. Ancient Art of the American Southwest*, which describes the elegant, stylized precision of their work, and how the decoraters: '*took intense delight in portraying themselves warmly integrated with rabbits, antelope, sunflowers – even bugs – of their landscape.*'

COLOUR, PATTERN AND FORM

Pattern contains the nature of nature.
Sōetsu Yanagi, *op. cit.*

Following Mimbres tradition, you can look to the natural world for inspiration – perhaps using modern microscopic photography which provides patterns from different scales and other worlds. I often use colour, patterns and form from living cell-structures such as chromosomes and 'nerve-ending' patterns, which come literally from inside myself. The intriguing diatoms, too, reveal exquisite forms, particularly suitable for work in porcelain (see page 12). Find further microscopic patterns in natural history books, such as *Plant Life In Miniature* by C. Postma.

On a larger scale there are strong forms from shells or patterns from tropical fish and you can visit geological and natural history museums to study colour, pattern and form in rocks, gems, shells and bone-structures.

Man-made forms can be an abundant source of patterns. Textiles, for example, have always inspired potters. Look, in particular, at the richness of design and colour in Kelim and oriental carpets; visit the patchworks in The American Museum, Claverton Manor, Bath, or read the admirable book, *African Textiles* by J. Pictold. And for forms, visit science museums to study the industrial machinery – particularly the cross-sections.

Try arranging objects randomly yourself to form the basis of a new design. Stained glass windows patched together from pieces of mediaeval glass have inspired my millefiori work. Kaleidoscopes can be an indispensible source of inspiration. Try either type: the one which has its coloured glass pieces inside with which to create pattern; or the other which you move about, and by a process of mirrors, transforms the world around you into a perpetually-renewable supply of designs.

Finally, try combinations of natural and industrially-made forms to produce a new vocabulary of form and expression. The potter, Geoffrey Swindell, manages this with fluency and polish, often combining press-moulding with fine hand-modelling. His natural shapes began to be influenced by his collection of tin toys. He says in *Potters on*

4 Swimming People. *Mimbres pot with spirit hole in centre. Height 12 cm (4¾in.); diameter 24 cm (9½in.)*

5 *Laser pattern. Centre section of a magnetic bubble film reduced by laser annealing*

Pottery, 'What I am looking for at the moment is a cross between organic forms and man-made forms. You find that, say, a speed boat and a fish are very closely related in structure, and I am trying to make an object now that achieves a synthesis of the two things without giving the immediate impression of a fish or a speed boat.'
See *page 14*.

6 Diatoms

PLACES TO FIND IDEAS

Perhaps the most directly accessible supply of valuable source material is to be found in museums. Use the heritage of museum treasure as a kick-off point for new work-ideas – not only the ceramics, but drawings, sculpture, jewellery, armour, etc. provide a constant flow of information. Do not neglect your local museums, which usually display excellent prehistoric and mediaeval pottery.

My favourite museums in Britain are the Ashmolean and Pitt Rivers in Oxford; The Fitzwilliam in Cambridge (be careful as the ceramics' section is open only at certain times); the British Museum, The Victoria & Albert, and The Museum of Mankind in London – though the last one tends to hide many of its treasures away. In America, have a look at the Peabody Museum, Boston, Heye Foundation, New York, and the museum at Santa Fé for American Indian pottery.

If you are abroad, try to see the Heraklion Museum, on Crete, where there are clay coffins shaped like tin-baths, great oil-storage jars, or the vividly-decorated pottery from Phaistos; the Musée Guimet in Paris, with its marvellous T'ang figures; and the Gulbenkian in Lisbon, where splendid examples of Hispano-Moresque ware are impeccably displayed. Further afield is the Calcutta Museum with Mohenjodaro and Indus Valley Civilization pottery and figurines. Finally, there are all the museums in and around Osaka, in Japan, where you can see the work of Koetsu and Kenzan, as well as prehistoric Jōmon ware.

7 Spouted vessel. Impressed and carved vessel, from Japan, late Joman period. Height 17.5 cm (7 in.). (Courtesy of the British Museum)

SYMBOLISM

One reason to visit museums is to look for pottery used for votive offerings. The ancient Egyptians, for example, visualized the next world as a mirror image of their own and were therefore concerned with the material well-being of departed souls. They included items to accompany the dead that were images of material possessions to sustain them on their journey and to be enjoyed in the next world. These offerings needed only to symbolize the real thing, because by magic, the representational models could be animated to serve the deceased's spirit. As

8 Porcelain form, Geoffrey Swindell, 1973. Made by a combination of moulding and hand building and inspired by the combination of organic and man-made structures. Diameter 8 cm (3 in.)

9 Earring figure, from Cyprus, late Bronze Age. Base ring ware. Height 21 cm (8 in). (Courtesy of Desmond Morris)

well as an abundance of food being represented, a wealthy person might have had models of his servants brewing and baking – even a working potter was sometimes depicted so that the deceased could be supplied with pottery for the life ahead.

This symbolic role of ceramics was prevalent in many primitive societies. Fertility symbols were particularly common, such as those from Cyprus or the Indus valley civilizations or the Willendorf Venus from Germany or the mother goddesses from Malta.

Wish-fulfillment is still very much alive today in countries like Mexico, where large American cars are fashioned from clay, painted bright pastel pink or blue and sold to customers so that one day they might own the real thing. Children display similar qualities. For a child, image and desire is more important than function. When playing with Plasticine or clay a child does not ask 'what is it for?; but 'what is it to be?' This desire to make an animal or person is all part of a primitive wish-fulfillment within us.

When taking up ceramics, you as a potter should have the same desire to make something personal. It is a good idea to start off by holding a piece of clay in your hands and shaping it into something remembered from childhood. We were given this exercise on our first day at the Royal College of Art,

London. I remembered making some doll-figures which my father helped me bake in the bottom of the bonfire, so I made some of these out of 'crank' clay (see page 79), which was the nearest thing to the clay marl I had dug from the garden so long ago. Another student modelled his memory of the blue and cream bus in which he travelled to school. Everyone's clay results made a personal and unique statement.

It is this that I would like to urge you to remember when reading this book. Collect pebbles; go to galleries, exhibitions, libraries; pin postcards around your working area; prop open books of beautiful pots. These will serve only as inspiration; when you are about to make your own, try not to copy other people's pottery – close your eyes and make it come from within. This does not mean that you cannot analyze other people's ceramics. Think about why you like them or what makes them work, then apply what you have learnt to your own pots. Even the greatest originators have emerged from a continuing tradition.

10 Skirt, Vanessa Pooley, 1988. 'T' Material with pieces cut and excavated. Height 51 cm (20 in.)

CHAPTER TWO

AESTHETICS

RHYTHM OR TENSION LINES

It is difficult to describe what makes the shape of a pot work. I believe that 'rhythm lines' which connect one part of the pot with another, together with the balance of volume (both inside and outside the pot) determine whether form and proportion work together. A rhythm line may give tautness to the vertical silhouette of the pot as the line springs from the base up to the rim; or on the horizontal silhouette, where it may follow the widest point of the pot, which itself may echo the silhouette of base and rim.

VOLUME

Volume, although not seen, is very definitely sensed. On a good pot, below its surface-texture and decoration, the tautness of volume can be felt pushing from the inside against the outer walls, like a blown-up paper bag. This is what forms a full and vigorous silhouette. On the fat, neolithic pot illustrated on page 17, the swirling decoration, whilst echoing the pot's form, seems almost to celebrate visually its inner volume, 'embracing' the swelling beneath. The two lugs placed on the widest part of the inflection only emphasize the tautness further, so that the pot appears pleased with itself.

Try out the 'paper-bag' test on a pot. Close the top opening of a pot except for a hole to blow through. The pot should still have damp, flexible walls, which will respond to your breath and fill out. Seal the hole quickly with a knob of clay and leave the pot to dry leather-hard before you open the top and finish it. The internal volume of this type of pot pushing outwards may be complemented by sharp indentions or concave areas where the force of air outside the pot is, so to speak, pushing in. If these two forces balance, your pot will have poise.

An excellent exercise to improve your awareness of working with volume and compensatory balance, is to tie circles of string tightly round various levels of a damp pot. Now reach inside and pinch out the clay on either side of the taut string until these areas are stretched to a full curve. In a way, it is the string here that is controlling the tension or rhythm lines, depending on where you have chosen to tie them.

Another way to involve space is by considering a group of pots. Experiment with their positioning in relation to each other and the space this generates. Elizabeth Fritsch specializes in trying to give shape to this space, and writes in the magazine *New Ceramics*, '*the space* between *pots assembled in groups (whether side by side or overlapping into the distance) is to me more lively and musical than any of the spatial relationships which may be incorporated in an individual piece.*'

CHANGE OF DIRECTION

Bernard Leach said that in pottery, '*Vertical lines are of growth, horizontal lines are of rest, diagonal lines are of change.*'

Where you are changing from a convex to a concave shape or vice versa, make the transition definite, because the eye will quickly pick up 'slackness' in the connecting

space. In a way, there should be no 'in between' stage from one shape to another; each shape should flow. If you want a flat area, think of this as being stretched between the two forms on either side so that you will not interrupt the lines of energy. If you do this, you will never form a slack area unintentionally. Continuity is obviously much more difficult to obtain on a hand-built pot than on a thrown one where the fingers are always pushing tautly against the centrifugal force. Phillip Rawson describes this well in his book, *Ceramics*:

Whereas the surface of a thrown pot may be described as the mechanical function of revolution of an unchanged line, the surface of a modelled pot can only be achieved as an invented sequence of continually changing lines. This means that in a modelled pot the transitions from one grip to another on horizontal circuits of the pot must be calculated as carefully as those on the vertical axis.

A change of direction can produce troughs and ridges, the widest or deepest points of which may be used positively as good horizontal or vertical tension lines. You could emphasize these further by allowing glaze to

11 Funerary urn. Neolithic earthenware, from Ginsu Bensham, West China, 2500 BC. (Courtesy of the trustees of the British Museum)

· 17 ·

collect in a trough or rubbing oxides in; whilst on the ridges, use glaze thinly, to contrast these areas with those above and below.

WHETHER A POT 'WORKS'

There are no fixed rules for proportion, but one relationship which invariably works is the 'Golden Section', where the proportion of A to B is one third more or two thirds more than the proportion B to C. Whether using fixed proportion or not, always remember to be aware of the whole form and not just the part you are concentrating on.

Whether a pot 'works' depends upon various criteria:
- Does it feel right?
- Is it pleasing to the eye? Has it strength of expression?
- Are form, proportion, surface and decoration working as one?
- And are they all going towards describing the pot's own character?

I believe that a good pot draws a reaction from you like a gasp or a smile. It is giving out something from itself that makes you want to look at it again. Certainly some pots that have lasted through history give the feeling that they possess a kind of magic quality together with a 'timelessness'. This is something to work towards achieving today.

Ultimately a pot 'works' when all the parts

enhance one another. If one part fails to do this, the whole pot will look wrong. Often the areas that don't work are ones you had trouble with – just as areas that do work are invariably achieved with ease. You can step back and review your handiwork rationally but it is the inspiration from within that gives true creation. Many potters find pinching a pot the most introspective of all ceramic methods; some even pinch with their eyes closed . . . in that way the shaping of the clay really comes from within. The first method shown will be to form a pinch pot; but before that, you must choose your clay and observe a few rules on technique.

12 Composite vase with white glaze and floral decoration, from Sesebi, New Kingdom, Egypt, c.1300 BC (Courtesy of the trustees of the British Museum)

CHAPTER THREE

CLAYS

The transformation of this muddy substance into a sort of stone is almost magical. Clay particles are thin and flat, rather like scales. When combined with water, however, they become malleable, and in this state clay can be made into a myriad of shapes. After being dried the clay is fired to a temperature that allows it to harden and be preserved. With the addition of a glaze it becomes non-porous and will hold water or store perishable goods. It can be a thing of beauty in its own right, not only to look at, but to hold and touch, imparting to whoever does so some of the experience that its maker felt at its creation. Clay can be wrinkled, pulled, pinched, moulded, folded, wrapped, coiled or kept flat. It has limitless possibilities, but to give of its best, needs careful preparation.

I hope to show not only the ordinary uses of the material for hand-building, but how it can be pushed to the edge of these limits. I will give ideas, suggest experiments, throw in some tips, point out ways to get the best use from it – and how to avoid pitfalls. In this way excitement, exploration and discovery are combined with a few sensible rules.

13 Rock formation, from west Scotland. (Photo: Jane Waller)

Bernard Leach says wisely in *A Potter's Book*, '*It is far better to run the occasional risk of making an occasional blunder than to attempt cold-blooded analyses based upon other people's theories.*' So, although techniques and ideas are given, experiment and explore for yourself.

There are three main rules for the technique of hand-building:

1 The clay must be in the right condition for what you want to make. If it is too soft, the object – unless held in a mould or a cloth – will collapse from lack of structure; if it is too hard, it will break like a biscuit.

2 Separate pieces of clay added together must be joined properly. Failure to do so will cause cracking during drying or firing.

3 Dry your clay shape slowly and evenly or it will warp or crack. Ideally clay should be the same thickness throughout, so if your walls are of differing widths, take care to keep thinner areas damp while thicker parts begin to dry out. Instructions for doing this are shown below.

Fine clays take longer to dry than those coarsened with the addition of pre-shrunk materials such as grog or sand. Likewise, a closed form will take longer than an open one; in an open form, thin rims should be dried more slowly by being covered in damp strips of newspaper or cloth and/or polythene. To prevent drafts affecting the

14 *Jar with bridged spout. Red clay with impressed design, and covered with a thin black wash, from Palaikastro, Crete, late Minoan period.* (Courtesy of the trustees of the British Museum)

drying process, make a polythene tent to put the form under. Your work will be ready to bisque-fire without any danger of exploding in the kiln when the surface feels dry and slightly warm to the touch. Pots decrease in weight by about 10 per cent during drying and firing. If you added a non-shrinking material such as sand, quartz, talc, flint or grog to the clay, the total weight loss will be less. During firing, at around 100°C (212°F), there is a loss of some 30 per cent of free water, and at around 600°C (1112°F), from 3 to 13 per cent of chemically combined water evaporates and changes the clay irreversibly.

TYPES OF CLAY

Choose a clay suitable for what you want to make. You will acquire this knowledge through experience and will be able to build your own storehouse of information, discovering the strong, cement-like quality of Crank or 'T' Material, the plasticity of earthenware or stoneware, or learning to manage the more difficult but compelling qualities of porcelain. Clay is not simply one material but an infinitely variable class of types. I am only describing the main ones. For more information Kenneth Clark's *The Potter's Manual* is an excellent book to consult on clays.

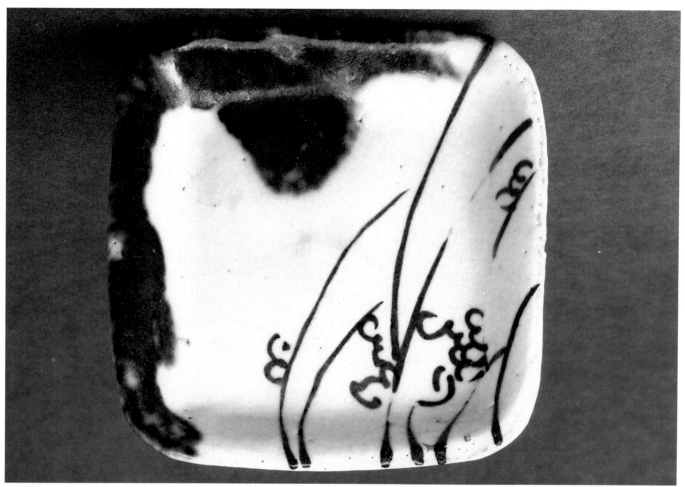

15 Square pickle dish decorated with green, white and brown enamels, from Japan, Edo period.
Length 1.07 m (42 in.). (Courtesy of the British Museum)

RED EARTHENWARE

The warm, reddish colour of red earthenware comes from a content of 8 to 10 per cent of iron oxide. It is particularly good for slabbing, coiling and burnishing. It is excellent for decorating when covered first with a coloured or white slip. Firing temperatures are between 900 and 1080°C (1652 and 1976°F) according to type. The low-temperature glaze required for this clay forms a skin over the bisqued body, and the colours remain bright.

WHITE EARTHENWARE

This clay has medium plasticity and is perfect for staining with colour. Although its firing range is between 1060 and 1180°C (1940 and 2156°F), if the clay is bisqued to 1140°C (2084°F) and glazed at earthenware temperatures, colours do not fire away. It can be fired to vitrification temperature without the need of a glaze. (Vitrification is when the clay itself becomes fused as a non-porous mass.)

STONEWARE

Stoneware has a dense, non-porous, stone-like quality, and most stoneware clays are suitable for coiling, slabbing and pinching. At the clay's firing range, 1200–1300°C (2192–2372°F), according to type, the glaze is fused into the body. Stoneware can be fired unglazed to vitrification point using coloured oxides. In a reduction firing, glazes undergo exciting colour changes (Reduction is the process whereby clay is fired in an oxygen-reduced atmosphere).

PORCELAIN

Porcelain is formed from china clay, feldspar or Cornish stone, with a little ball clay added for plasticity. It is good for pinching but has a critical moisture-range and can easily become too soft or too dry to work. It can be opaque or translucent according to thickness and glazing, and has a high firing-temperature of 1280–1300°C (2336–2372°F). When combined with grog, porcelain can be used for raku.

MIXED CLAYS

Today's clays are all refined, so experiment by mixing different types together. Different clays can be mixed as long as they have the same shrinkage rate or are 'opened' and strengthened with grog, sand, etc. to accommodate the degree of stress. For example:

- A marbling effect can be obtained if two clays of the same type but of different tone are wedged together; or if one body is used and half of it stained a different colour with an oxide or body-stain.
- Earthenware clay normally has a firing range of up to 1060–1080°C (1940–1976°F), but it can be fired to stoneware temperatures if it is 'opened' with the addition of grog or sand.

GROGS

Fireclay grog is a high refractory clay found close to coal seams. After being fired to a high temperature, it is then ground to different grades of coarseness, from a gritty texture to a fine powder. Having thus been 'preshrunk', it is added to clay to help prevent shrinkage and impart strength.

Molochite is a white grog – a china clay vitrified and ground to a range of sizes from coarse to dust. I have found that molochite has a good stabilizing effect that prevents stained clays used side by side from cracking, for example, in the millefiori process (chapter 11).

Commercial clays that have grog in them, like Crank, are excellent for all kinds of clay work where strength is desired, for the grog imparts a more open texture to the clay allowing thicker walls to be built. 'T' Material, which has molochite in it, is excellent for the same reasons; in addition, being white, it is also good for colour work. It is, however, expensive.

RAKU CLAYS

Open rough clays that withstand sudden thermal shock are necessary for rakuing. Crank and 'T' Material as well as other commercial clays specially prepared for raku are readily obtainable and excellent. You can also make your own grogged clays. Porcelain when mixed with molochite can be used for raku, and provides a good body for colour staining etc. Stoneware, too, can be used, mixed with grog. Firing is from 750 to 1000°C (1382–1832°F).

FOUND CLAY

It is an exciting and rewarding experience to dig your own clay. Impurities left in the body produce colour and tone variation, which make a very individual clay. If your found clay is sticky, temper it with some sand or 30 to 40 per cent talc.

PREPARING FOUND CLAY

1 Pull the clay into small pellets and allow to dry.

2 Drop them into a bucket a third filled with water, allowing the pellets to soak up as much water as they want, adding more water if necessary.

3 The following day, after the pieces have slaked, mix to a slip by hand before putting the whole lot through a coarse sieve to remove sticks, stones and other debris.

4 Now your clay is levigated, dry it on plaster bats until it can be wedged into balls.

5 Wrap each ball tightly in soft polythene then store them in a plastic dustbin. (All clay improves by keeping, as its plasticity is increased – so the longer, the better.)

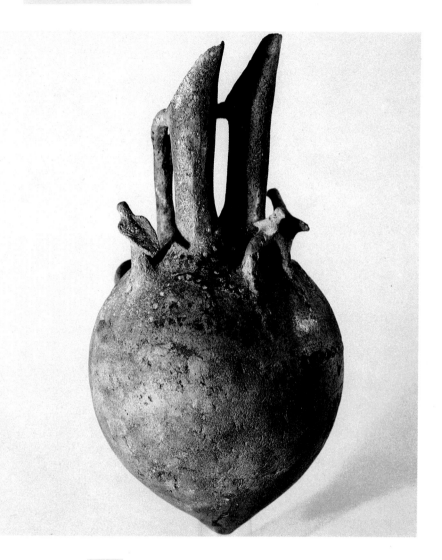

16 Twin-necked jug with pointed base and beak spouts. Drab polished ware from Crete, Middle Bronze Age. Height 38.5 cm (15 in.). (Photo: Desmond Morris; courtesy of the Desmond Morris collection)

You can make tests to see how much your clay shrinks and what you have to add to improve the texture – three per cent of ball clay or bentonite will, for example, make the clay more plastic. I added 150 g ball clay and a little sand to 1000 g of clay dug out of my cellar. I bisque-fired my found-clay pots to 1000°C (1832°F), then sawdust-fired them (Chapter 8). The differing tones in the clay varied from warm brick reds through to yellows, greys and a smoky dark grey where carbon was deposited from the firing.

TIP

If you discover a white bloom of salts of lime appearing on your found clay after it is fired, an addition of 1 per cent barium chloride will neutralize this.

WEDGING

Wedging ensures that the clay is sufficiently plastic. When kneaded, the flat particles of clay lie close together in parallel lines, thus increasing the molecular attraction and therefore the plasticity. The whole lump is homogenously damp, air bubbles are expelled and any foreign matter can be removed as it is revealed. I wedge by the spiral method, cutting the clay through in two or three places every so often to check the state inside.

METHOD

Wedging is done using your whole body, the weight and pressure passing downwards through back, shoulders, arms and hands in a rhythmic movement. The heel of one hand is pushed hard into the clay while the other hand turns the clay round little by little. The hand that is pushing down is always over the concave centre, landing just below the previous wedge. The spiral pattern that develops is like that of a fossil ammonite or a chrysanthemum petal. Slicing, looking inside to remove unwanted material – especially long hairs in my case – thumping the clay together again and re-spiralling is carried out until the clay is clean inside and malleable, and the stickiness has gone. Now it is ready to use.

PREPARATION TIPS

Before you start work, here are some tips, which will lessen the risk of accidents both to you and to your ceramics.

- keep your work area uncluttered, and clean up after every session
- keep your tools clean, sharp and dry
- always have a clean wedging bat
- make sure your overalls and cloths are washed frequently
- keep your clay damp and clearly labelled
- make a note of all your experiments
- install an extractor fan in your work area and by your kiln, if possible
- always wear a mask if you are scraping and sanding, or working with anything powdered

CHAPTER FOUR

PINCHING A POT

A pinch pot can be as simple or as complex as you make it – a simple bowl or an asymmetric organic shape. The pincher has no wheel to help spin the clay into shape, no mould to force it into position. The shape of the clay is purely the result of each squeezing of thumb and finger while you cradle the pot in your hands.

Because this method gives complete intimacy with the clay, it is a good idea to start off by making a pinch pot. Besides, this must have been how the very first pot was made, and from a round ball of clay shaped rather like the primordial egg.

MATERIALS

BEGINNERS

Wedge up a lump of grogged clay. Being strong and cement-like in texture, this body will take virtually any shape without cracking. You could begin by making a votive offering, modelling a member of your family (with or without sticking pins in it!), or forming a fertility god. When dry, these could

be baked in the bottom of the fire grate or under the bonfire.

Next, using the method given below, you may want to pinch your own bowl. Even if this is thick-walled you can smooth over the rim. Then you could try to pinch thinly a cup to drink from. Pay attention to the rim. Will it feel comfortable to your lips? Will your hand fit nicely around the handle? Remember, clay shrinks, so make this larger than you want it to be.

EXPERIENCED POTTERS

More experienced potters will prefer stoneware or even porcelain to make a thinner-walled pot of refinement. I often use a 50/50 mix of 'T' Material and buff stoneware. (The smoother buff gives warmth to the rather dead white, but stronger 'T' Material).

METHOD

STARTING OFF

Get into a comfortable position in a quiet

place. Pinching a pot is a peaceful, introspective occupation. Better to be on your own perhaps with some inspiring music if you need your marginal attention filled. In summer I like to sit among my flowers; in the winter, in front of a fire. Wherever you work, it is difficult to make a pinch-pot whilst chatting – especially when you know that every pinch you make will alter the pot.

Rub barrier cream into your hands before starting. You will still feel the clay's texture, but your hands will not dry out. In addition, barrier cream protects against dangerous oxides entering the skin (Chapter 11). By the way, it is useless to pinch with long finger-nails – those will have to go.

Start with a ball of clay that is not too unwieldy and fits comfortably in the hand. Use clay that has just been wedged – or re-wedged if it has been wrapped in polythene – so that the surface is not drier than the interior. The clay should be of the same consistency, dampness and plasticity.

Pat it smooth, revolving it as you do so. Work out where you want the opening to be by pressing gently with your thumb as you turn until the opening begins to enlarge. Now work your way down to within 6–10 mm ($\frac{1}{4}$–$\frac{3}{8}$ in) for the pot's base – the base should be determined here as you may not be able to reach it later – then spread the opening sideways, turning the ball evenly as you do so. Having formed the bottom, you can start to pull the clay vertically, or into a hemisphere if you are making a bowl.

Now you must attend to the outer silhouette as these initial upward movements will give spring from the base. Change the pressure: use your outside fingers to press against the inside thumb if you want to go straight up, or push more with your thumb from the inside against your outside fingers if you want to travel out.

Stroke the clay, drawing it in the chosen direction, or pinch with minute pinches of even pressure, turning the pot a fraction for every movement you make. Now go round again, pinching the ridges between the pinches you have made before. You will find as you work that the clay seems to slide and soften under your fingers, becoming more plastic as you work. Use the hand that isn't pinching as a support and to move the pot round and round like a very slow-moving wheel. Like a turning wheel make this action smooth – jerky movements will stretch the pot and be reflected in its walls. Make sure you complete a full revolution, pinching one particular movement all the way round so that the walls get the same amount of 'stretch' and stay an even thickness.

TIP 1

Often, the rim will crack and has to be mended. Stroke clay over the crack from either side until it is healed. Cracking can be prevented if you keep the rim sloping inwards. (It can always be opened later.) Also, it is a good idea to keep the rim fat and rounded, so, when you make your stroking movements from the base, stop short before you reach the rim, (I moisten my rims with saliva every so often to dampen them – it's not as 'wet' as water and therefore does not weaken the rim.)

TIP 2

When you feel the walls going limp and floppy, **stop immediately**. Rest the work rim downwards on a cushion of foam or several layers of polythene, so that this part, which consists of clays you haven't yet worked, stays damp. A bowl can be formed in a few minutes, but it will be heavy, flaccid, lumpy and thick, probably splitting at the rim and with no tension in its walls. As such, a child's pinch pot will have an endearing artless quality, but an adult's! If you are an impatient worker, pinch two or even three pots simultaneously so while one is firming up, you start forming the next.

By holding the pinch-pot sideways as you work, you can constantly check the vertical silhouette; so pause every so often to look at the horizontal one. I often reinforce the pot's shape at this stage by stroking over the pinching with my thumb, bringing the clay up, as well as around, both outside and inside. With this direct contact of thumb, fingers and clay, it is easy to feel how thin the walls are becoming, how taut the shape is, or whether the pot is getting too limp and needs to dry a little before continuing.

RIMS

Once the pot has firmed up, you will be able to work on the fat, inward-sloping rim. Pinch this out into a simple bowl-shape and smooth the final rim over with first the fingers and then a damp chamois-leather. Or change direction, pinching inwards or outwards. Alternatively, pinch the rim into an irregular shape and leave it smooth or textured.

TIP 3

Beginners often make mistakes with feet and rims. This is because they think of them as appendages. 'What shall I do when I reach the rim?' is not the right approach. The rim and foot should seem to grow out of the pot, pushing out into space, celebrating everything in the form that has led up to – or down to – them.

FINISH

Once completed, dry the pinch pot under loose polythene if it is thin-walled; if thicker and made from grogged clay, it will probably dry without harm uncovered, away from direct heat.

At the leather-hard stage, you can work on the pot further by scraping and refining the shape with a metal kidney. Be prepared for some scratching from heavily-grogged clay – this can be quite attractive, however, when the dragged grooves follow the rhythm of scraping, which itself is related to the shape of the pot. Finally, work over the pot with one of those scratchy kitchen scourers or sandpaper – don't forget to wear a mask when you do this.

TIP 4

A slight depression made in the centre of the base will allow the pot to stand securely.

EXPERIMENTS

1 Make a really thick pot, then carve shapes out of it.

2 Change the symmetry. Check whether your asymmetrical pot will stand without falling over and that it has a strong 'centre' of balance, even if this is not at the pot's centre. *See* fig. 20 page 35.

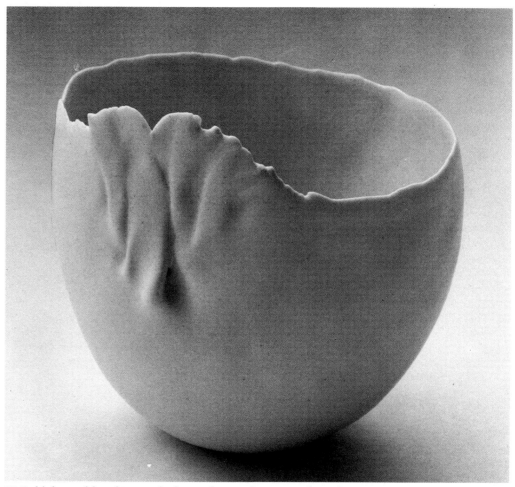

17 Fold-fronted bowl in pinched porcelain with a matt white glaze, Mary Rogers. 10 × 10 cm (4 × 4 in.)

3 Change the rim. Make it irregular, organic: swoop it up into a funnel-shape or two funnel-shapes (*see* fig. 16, page 23).

4 Try to pinch a very thin pot. You may want to try porcelain at this stage.

PORCELAIN

Very delicate shapes, frills, folds, fossil-forms or diatom shapes can be pinched out of porcelain (see fig. 6). When using it, everything must be spotless. Any grain of foreign matter will spoil your work: so keep a set of rolling-pin, scalpel-knife, spatulas, etc. specially for porcelain. Use a piece of clean, white, heavy canvas or cotton duck as a working-surface.

Wedge the porcelain until it feels plastic and has lost some of its stickiness. Proceed as for pinching other clays – but form the base down to 3 mm ($\frac{1}{8}$ in) thick. You will find the whole 'feel' of porcelain different. To obtain those particularly delicate but taut thin walls, you must pinch porcelain evenly. It is vital to pinch for one round, then pinch the ridges in between those pinches on the next.

Squeeze only very gently until you have reached further up the pot, then when the clay has dried out a little, pinch with more pressure. The resting and firming-up periods, too, will be considerably shorter, as porcelain itself has a less plastic or 'short' consistency and will dry out faster, especially as you are pinching it thinner. Patience, a soft touch and

careful handling will reward your efforts.

When you are not working, rest your pot on a low-sided cloth-covered yoghurt pot, or on a piece of soft foam inside an old plaster mould.

RIMS

Rims can be encouraged to curl, frill or split; or be rounded and smooth. The difficulty is to catch the porcelain at the right plasticity for shaping the rim before this dries. Don't wet the clay but perhaps damp your fingers down a little if the rim is drying out. If you want the rim to travel inwards, draw clay up the outside of the form and over the rim, or, if needs be, make a tuck in the clay and pinch this well together.

FEET

A delicate form can be 'lifted' with the addition of a foot-ring; this can be added at the leather-hard stage. First rest the bowl on a rubber ball inside a yoghurt pot. (This can be eased out later). A piece of muslin draped over the ball first will stop it sticking. Next score the surfaces to be joined with a knife or toothbrush, then glue them with a smear of liquid clay. Place a small, extra coil of clay firmly into the join on the inside – and possibly on the outside, too. These extra coils can be eased in and smoothed over.

FINISH

Unlike other clays, porcelain is weaker and more liable to crack or bend at the leather-

hard stage, so wait until the work has dried harder. Then add tension to the form by carefully scraping the pot with a flexible metal kidney. The kidney will make better purchase at this stage, whereas at the leather-hard stage it would merely smudge the surface. Nevertheless, even at the harder stage, scraping must be done with the minimum pressure and maximum concentration. If you are jerky or hurried, fine porcelain work is not for you!

TRANSLUCENCY

Porcelain gains its translucency by having very thin walls. To do this either scrape all over, or etch a design through part of the wall. If you want to pierce the walls completely, use dental tools. (These can be ordered from Fulham Pottery and Alec Tiranti — *see Suppliers*.) Engraver's tools are also useful, or fine drill-bits. Piercing and carving porcelain is painstaking work, needing full concentration. Later, the carving can be gently smoothed with a *damp* sponge or chamois-leather.

Pinching is for small pots but becomes an unwieldy method for larger ones. Coiling may have been invented when pots larger than pinched ones were needed.

18 Porcelain pot with pierced holes and oxide decoration, Nicole Johns. (Photo: Bob Beasley; courtesy of Ceramic Review)

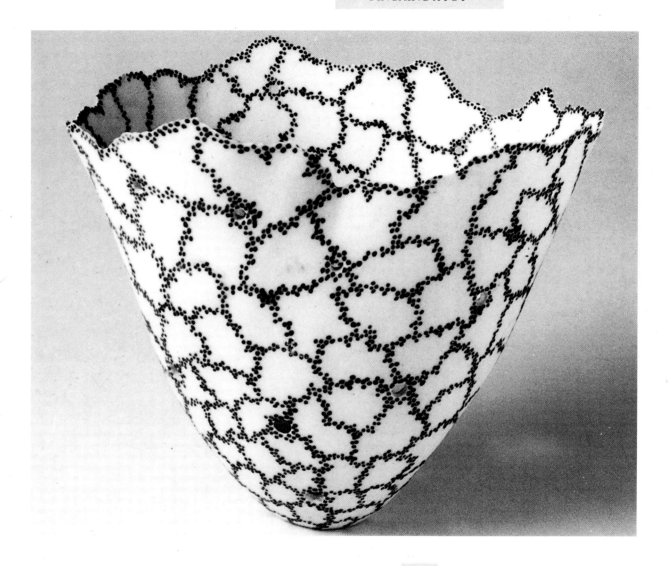

CHAPTER FIVE

COILING

Coiling is similar to basket-making. The pot is built by winding coils of clay horizontally rather than working in a vertical direction as in pinching or throwing. When coiling, therefore, it is the circumference that has to be constantly checked. This may be one of the reasons why many Africans are not seated when they coil their pots, but seem to dance round them as though *they* were the potter's wheel.

Use a turn-table so that you can turn the pot frequently to eye the vertical silhouette. If you place it on a stool instead of a table, this will allow you to stand over your work to check the horizontal silhouette.

Some think it unnecessary to coil a pot in a shape which you could make more quickly on the wheel, but because coil pots, by their very nature, **are** hand-made and constructed by a slower process than throwing, slight and inevitable differences occur around the silhouette. It is this that gives coiling its vigorous, exciting quality, and it is this that makes each coil pot unique. In a wheel-thrown pot, the quickly pulled-up silhouette is what the eye rests on, whereas on a coil pot, the eye moves with interest over an uneven surface – though this may be almost imperceptible.

SCALE

Coiling is perhaps the most versatile of ceramic methods. You can coil large or small. The great oil-storage jars of Crete were probably made by the islanders coiling ropes of clay about 5 cm (2 in) thick, which they added whilst walking backwards round the pot (see opposite). You could fill the kiln with an outsize pot – if you can afford it!

Conversely, delicate pots can be created using very thin coils. Jennifer Aamon (see page 33) has perfected this method, covering her smoothed-over coils with first a slip, then a painted design. Her rims are made by rolling the clay gradually over with her fingers, and the finish of her pots is excellent.

METHOD

WEDGING
Wedge up more than enough clay for the whole work. This ensures you have a consistent mix to draw from. Keep each wedged ball of clay wrapped tightly in soft polythene and put them inside a plastic bag. (You can mix a small quantity with water to make a clay slurry for joining coils together.)

While wedging, you could plan the pot you are going to make. Remember, with a coil pot it is important to know beforehand what shape you want. A well thought-out form will be stronger than an undetermined one. Uncertain coiling will show in the finished work.

THE BASE
Coils will tend to unwind during firing if they are used to make your pot's base, so instead use a rolled-out slab for the base – oval, round, or whatever your shape is to be. The base should be the same thickness as your coils. Place this base onto a piece of newspaper cut to its exact shape. Because

your clay is damp, the newspaper will hold, and it can stay there throughout the pot's creation, preventing it from sticking to the turntable. (The paper base will burn away in firing.)

Experienced potters begin their coiling by using a plaster mould – or a former made from a bisque-fired predetermined shape – to support that awkward area of clay wall from the base of the pot to the first few inches above. As well as ensuring the beginnings of a taut silhouette, the mould will suck water from the clay allowing it to firm up the bottom of your pot, ready to support the added coils above. (I stretch butter-muslin inside my former to prevent the pot sticking to the mould and so that I am able to lift the pot out easily at any time to check the continuity of the silhouette.) Only the pot's working rim is kept damp by using strips of wet newspaper and polythene so that the coils will join well. Formers are well worth using as they get your pot off to a really good start. They also ensure that your pot does not have that sagging, lifeless area so commonly seen just above the base.

19 *Large coiled storage jar from the Palace of Knossos, Crete, 1450–1400 BC. A coiled lip is turned over in a heavy roll and impressed moulding represents cord and rope patterns. Height 1.14 m (3 ft 8 in.). (Courtesy of the trustees of the British Museum)*

The Africans use a piece of concave gourd to put the clay into.

STARTING TO COIL
Some coilers prefer to roll out several coils first and wrap these, full-length, in polythene so that they can work uninterrupted. Others like the small space of time needed to roll a new coil while they consider their work.

I found making rounded coils difficult at first. Mine turned into flat shapes that thumped along the table, because the clay I was using was too hard. The secret is to roll out fairly damp coils using just your fingers in short movements, stretching the clay sideways along the coil.

Now score the rim of your base, which should still be damp. If it isn't, put a thin coat of slurry into the scoring before squeezing on your first coil, then join this thoroughly to the base. Coil away, and after each completed circle, push some clay from the new coil down over the one below and some up from this into your new coil. Do this both on the outside and inside so that the coils are well-knitted. This is important as the pot gets its structural strength from this and is unlikely to crack along a coil-join when fired. (Imogen Ward pinches the coil below into a V-shaped point, then wipes a little slurry onto the added coil before pushing it down on either side for a strong connection. See page 37.) Where one coil-end is joined to the next, both can be sliced diagonally, then scored, daubed with slurry, and overlapped, welding the clay together so that no trace of join remains.

Bulging

Coil pots have an inherent tendency to splay outwards; therefore, a wise precaution is to keep the top coil slanting inwards a little. With coiling it is much easier to push the walls outwards during the scraping period than to take up extra clay from an unwanted bulge. One method that will cure small bulges is to slap the area sharply with a wooden paddle whilst supporting the pot on the inside with your hand. (A paddle is a flat-sided

spatula; make one yourself, buy a suitable kitchen utensil, or modify a wooden spoon by sanding down the back.) Use a paddle to tighten and strengthen form throughout. With precise hitting movements you can flatten unwanted surface irregularities or purposefully make them for an asymmetrical pot.

Anvil and Paddle method

In many parts of the world an 'anvil' or smooth pebble is held against the pot's inside wall while the pot is beaten, thinned and formed with a wooden paddle outside – in a way similar to beating out metal. Time must be left for the pot-walls to harden off – though this will happen faster because the walls have been beaten thinner.

Depressions

If there is a slight depression in your pot's wall, use a cloth-covered pestle to tap gently from the inside whilst supporting the outside.

PROBLEMS

AVOIDING SAGGING

The common fault that beginners make is to carry on coiling beyond the point where the pot can support its own weight. In their eagerness to have the thing completed they will end up with sagging walls and find, to their dismay, that they are no longer in control.

If this happens, STOP! Even one coil more will be one too many. All the work done will be wasted. The tension goes, the rhythm lines disappear and the silhouette is destroyed. The best way to stop this happening is to finish coiling after every five rounds or so and level the working rim with a sharp blade. (You can gently spin the turn-table to mark the level with a needle before cutting.)

Now with your metal kidney or length of hacksaw blade, work over the part you have coiled. Scrape and press slightly, using sweeping movements over the vertical silhouette – right from the base to where you have coiled up to – also round the horizontal silhouette, turning the pot as you go. You can combine both vertical and horizontal scraping if you work upwards in a spiral, especially if you are standing and your pot rests on a stool.

Because your movements echo and reassess the silhouette you have already made, your pot should now be a taut shape right to the ground. (African coilers rest their pots, many of which are round-based, on woven rafia rings, so that they can reach right to the base with each rhythmic scrape. By standing, they can really lift with every movement. Again, stopping coiling to scrape is worth doing, as not only does it neaten and re-define the pot's outline, but gives you a clearer picture of which direction to place your next set of coils. More important, it has compressed and spread the clay evenly, consolidating your coils, making your pot stronger. The inside,

Coil pot, Jennifer Aamon. Decorated with coloured slips and oxides. 12 × 10 cm (4¾ × 4 in.)

too, can be neatened so that you don't have to stretch down to do this later. Add no further coils until the pot has firmed up. Wait!

If the above procedure is followed, your pot will always have *lift* and never *sag*. It is taking this extra trouble that makes the difference between a good potter and an indifferent one. A hurriedly-made pot will look hurriedly made. A considered, strongly-structured pot will look well.

(For African coil pots, see Mary Roger's book *On Pottery and Porcelain*)

CHANGES OF DIRECTION

When you reach a point in your pot where you need to travel sharply outwards or inwards, allow the coils below to firm up more than usual, to take the extra load of coils being placed onto the outer or inner edge. If you are impatient, it is better to have two coil pots on the go. While one is drying, work on the other. This has the added advantage of your being able to re-assess the shape of your first pot when you return to it.

RIMS

If your pot is large, a thick, bold coil could be placed on the rim and left rounded, oval, ledged outwards, curled over, curled inwards – whatever suits the pot's shoulder and dimensions. On smaller coil pots the same could be done on a corresponding scale; or rims could be pinched thinner if you want a delicate finish. On all pot sizes, soft coils –

TIP

A good time to slice your working-rim level is when you are about to make a sharp change of direction. This ensures that the change is firm and even around the pot. I find this a good place and time to leave the work to firm up so that the slanting newly-added coils are well supported from below. Always keep the working-rim covered with strips of damp newspaper and polythene when you are not working on it.

---

maybe even differently-coloured ones – could be added plaited or twisted together.

If you have a simple, classic shape, it often looks good to keep the rim simple to match. If you want to add interest, you might give your pot handles, lugs, ridges, irregular rims, serrated rims, smooth organic rims, extraordinary rims, and so on. . . You could almost close the rim over – or completely over – but you will have to pierce two or three pin-sized air-holes so that your pot won't explode in the kiln.

Try adding sculpture to your pot around the rim. On my favourite pot from Phaestos, Crete, white daisies are modelled to stand proud of the surface (see page 60). On ancient Cypriot pots, small birds and animals were placed, or tiny figures pressed against the walls: even smaller pots were modelled, rising

---

from the surface like little cake-stands. These were ritual pieces placed in the grave of a departing soul, and although humans were meant never to see them again, the pottery still had to be of a high aesthetic quality in order to honour the dead as well as performing the practical function of carrying sustenance for the long journey to the other world (see illustrations on pages 23 and 61). Maybe you could invent a clay-mythology of your own?

TIP

I often neaten rims by squeezing and rubbing them into shape through slightly-dampened butter muslin. The marks made by the cloth are sometimes attractive enough to be left.

COIL FOOT-RINGS

If you intend to add a foot to your pot, make sure the base dries out to no more than leather-hard. If the foot is left until the rim is complete, both can be related to one another as well as to the silhouette between. Try joining the foot to the base while the pot is upside down; in this way you can observe all proportions objectively, considering the width, length and slant – if there is to be one on the foot-ring.

Another idea is to make several rough shapes and hold your pot onto them, or ask somebody else to do this, so that you can decide from afar. Mark and connect the leather-hard foot-ring securely, scoring and glueing the joining-place with slurry. A coil of clay worked inside where the ring joins the pot's base will strengthen the connection.

DRYING

Dry your pot under loose polythene and subsequently in the open. Make sure that the surface is dry and warm to the touch before bisqueing your pot to 1000°C (1832°F). Alternatively, it could be first slip-covered whilst still leather-hard, or burnished and sawdust-fired. (See Chapters on decoration.)

ALTERNATIVE METHODS OF COILING

Some potters prefer to build a pot using overlapping petals or circles of clay. Each petal is pressed together behind or in front of the ones below as well as overlapping sideways with its neighbour. This kind of wasp's nest pattern can be left on the outside as decoration – though it is better to smooth the inside over to strengthen the pot.

20 Swinging vessel, *Ewen Henderson, 1986. Laminated clays. Height 5 cm (2 in.). (Photo: David Cripps)*

Sometimes a pot is made using strips of clay cut from a rolled-out slab (see *Asymmetry* below).

COMPOSITE POTS

Two coil pots can be joined rim to rim; or wheel-thrown pots, when still leather-hard, can be extended with coiled areas, have added feet and spouts, or get squeezed asymmetrically with coiled areas added. Hans Coper used this with great success and his pots' proportions are especially good to study.

Pinch pots can be enlarged with coiled additions – but use the same batch of clay. Extra coils should be only slightly fatter than the parent-wall so that they can be pinched to a similar thickness. If the pot is to be rakued, then the coils will have to be extremely well pinched together, or cracking will occur along the joins.

ASYMMETRY

Asymmetry in coil pots is as tricky as it is for a pinch pot. To make the structure work is a question of weight, balance and volume control. Uneven-shaped or uneven-surfaced pots can have great presence if they are well-sculpted and well-balanced. Study Ewen Henderson's pots for their volume and form. Their asymmetry is a strange contradiction of movement and fossilization – as if the energy put into making the pot has been trapped inside (see page 35). They also contain a very strong inner space which pushes energetically against the wall's rugged skin. Ewen Henderson makes his decoration part of the structure. This quality of variety in texture and colour only emphasizes his pots' delightful irregularities, making them look like moon-craters or meteorites from outer space.

As his working method seems to be a cross between coiling and assembling a slab pot, this makes him a suitable person to use as a bridge to the next chapter. He works by rolling different clays into coils with inclusions of glaze stain, body stain, silicon carbide and opacifiers; then he flattens these out to build his forms. But owing to the mixtures of clay shrinking at different rates, these pots would often split, although they were joined with slurry. So now he laminates them onto a central body of stoneware, and assembles these in slabbed areas.

Large bowl, Imogen Ward, 1986. Coiled, burnished earthenware, open-fired in sawdust. 30.5 × 16.5 cm (12 × 6½ in.)

CHAPTER SIX

SLABBING

There are two different types of slabbing: soft-slabbing and hard-slabbing. Soft clay is responsive, yielding easily to bending, folding, crumpling and frilling. Soft-slabbing is similar to origami or dress-making: like origami, a definite decision has to be made before each handling of the clay, or the form will lose its crispness; like dress-making, the seams must be joined meticulously or they will come undone during drying or firing. Hard-slabbing is similar to joinery. Half-dried slabs of clay are butted together, glued with clay-cement, then the edges neatly planed. A hard-slabber must set out to be precise with measurements, tidy and ordered in construction and fastidious as to finish.

HARD-SLABBING

Two points should be noted before working with hard slabs:

- The preparation of the slabs is best done the day before, because these will need time to harden up evenly.

- Clay dislikes being flat, so grogged bodies are preferable for strength and to prevent warping in the drying and firing.

MAKING THE SLABS

Wedge up a fair amount of clay – you will need more than you think. Keep one ball aside for the present, well-wrapped in polythene.

Work out how many slabs you want, making them larger in area than you need. First, roll your clay blankets to about 12 mm ($\frac{1}{2}$ in) thick, on a piece of canvas placed on a smooth flat surface. Then, taking two straight battens of wood of the exact thickness you want your final slabs to be, lay these on either side of your blanket. Now roll with your rolling-pin along the top of the battens until the clay is level with them. Using slabs of the same thickness will prevent unsightly walls and uneven drying.

Alternatively, first wedge your clay into a block, then make two wooden posts of approximately 5 × 5 cm (2 × 2 in), marking off the thickness you want your slabs to be on each post all the way down, marking them level on each post. Stretch a piece of brass wire between the posts, winding it round each of your top markings. Now draw this through the clay block to cut your first slab down from the top of the block. Pushing downwards with the posts helps to keep the pulling level. Move the wire downwards progressively, cutting each slice against its measurement. This method is good for making small boxes. You may want to leave the texture made by the wire as a fresh-looking surface.

DRYING THE SLABS

Make all your slabs together, with extra for safety. Store these overnight, building them into a stack by first putting each slab between a page of newspaper, then a flat wooden board or piece of rigid perspex. (Better still, use a flat new kiln-shelf and no paper.) This is to ensure flat, even drying. If the walls are worked on too soft, or not dried completely flat, they will buckle, and continue to do so during firing.

When the slabs are dry enough to stand without buckling, yet still retain flexibility (just beyond leatherhard) you can start your construction. For making a box, cut one wall using a fine scalpel-knife against a transparent plastic ruler, then use this wall as a template for its opposite. Plastic set-squares and T-squares are useful tools to correct angles. Having rolled out slabs larger than required, you can now cut your box walls from the middle of each piece where the clay has dried consistantly and is flat.

TIP

Cut your slabs first from both ends, then the middle. This ensures that the corners won't snap . . . because you are working the clay drier than usual.

TIP

If you are butting the slabs together, remember to allow extra length for your overlaps. Decide, too, whether you want the walls to stand on the base or be fixed to the base's side, and allow for this extra thickness in the ground-plan. I generally stand the walls on the base as this helps to pull the walls in and prevent cracking at the joins. I can also reach the edges more easily to neaten them. If you cut the base last, you can make allowance for the walls not being dead on square.

JOINING THE SLABS
To join the slabs, unwrap a little of the soft clay put aside in polythene, and dilute to a slurry for the glue. First, thoroughly score each area to be joined with a criss-cross pattern. Then paste both seams and press well together. Wipe away excess squeezed-out slurry. As they are joined, the walls can be supported against bricks and flat pieces of board.

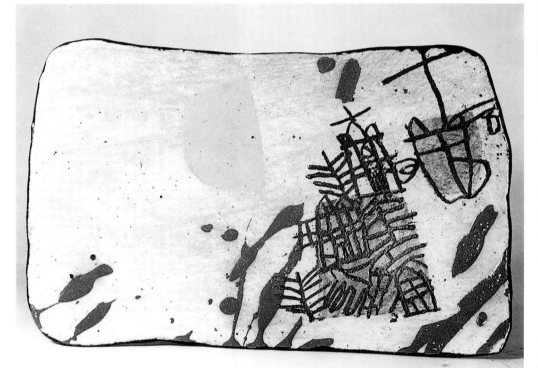

21 Small sea-port, Suffolk, John Maltby. Slab-built dish (oxidized). 32.5 × 23 cm (13 × 9 in.)

Slide joining

Another joining method is to score and wipe the seams to be joined with a little water. Repeat this process a second time, then slide the two walls from side to side to produce slip from the clay walls themselves. Do this until a secure grip is felt. This should be done neatly and precisely.

TIP

If you are overlapping the slabs, leave a fraction of the overlapping wall proud of the end. You can always shave this neatly away, whereas if the overlap is a fraction too short you will be in trouble.

FORTY-FIVE DEGREE CHAMFERING

Instead of overlapping, slabs can be joined by first placing them flat against the edge of the table and with a surform, chamfering the edges to 45 degrees. (I take the surform-blade from its holder so that it is less unwieldy and gives more control.) The chamfered slabs are first scored, then basted with slurry – this slightly softens the thinned edges and enables you easily to connect them by sliding your

22 Harbour with boat and net, John Maltby. Decorated with white earthenware glaze. Height 23 × 23 cm (9 × 9 in.)

finger and thumb along the outer walls in one firm sweep.

FINISH

When you have joined your four walls to the base, an excellent way to finish is to roll some small, even coils kept aside from the softer clay, and run these along every seam on the inside of your box. With one finger, press a coil well into the angle of the wall, holding a ruler against the outer wall for support. Leave the concave depression that your finger makes naturally, so that after you have cleaned away excess clay from either side of this seam, you are left with a rounded inner 'skirting', which strengthens and softens the way one wall runs into the other. It looks neat, too, and is easier to keep clean in use.

The finished joints can be levelled with a surform and smoothed using a kitchen scourer – although with a well-made overlapped box, you may want to leave the joint showing as decoration.

TIP

When making larger boxes, you can cut spacers from the extra clay slabs, which, being of the same batch and dampness, will shrink at the same rate. Place these to keep the box's inner walls straight while drying and firing.

23 Fan box decorated in Kenzan style with formal patterns and a flowering branch, from Japan, seventeenth century. 9 cm (3¾ in.). (Courtesy of the trustees of the British Museum)

24 *Prehistoric slabbed sarcophagus. Terracotta, decorated with soft yellow slip and painted patterns, from Palaikastro, Crete. 22 × 28.5 × 16.5 cm (8½ × 11 × 6½ in.).*
(Courtesy of the trustees of the British Museum)

FEET

If you are making a tall, thin box, it is attractive to add a narrow foot under the base. This will visually lift the pot by casting a shadow beneath, emphasize the form above and appear to lighten its weight.

LIDS

Lids, like bases, can be left until last so that you can tailor them to your finished shape. To prevent the lid sliding off the box, give it a small ledge to fit it nicely inside. I generally construct the small ledge first, matching it to the inside of the box. Then I place the lid on the box and scratch a line with a needle under where the lid touches the outer walls. This gives me the exact position behind which I can glue the ledge to the lid. Fit one of the small coils along the inside of the ledge, smoothing it concave like the rest of the seams. Then stick a piece of newspaper wherever the lid touches the box when in position and fit the lid on. Now true up the lid edges to match the outer walls, and leave it to dry in place to shrink with the rest of the box. If you dry the box on its lid there will be less chance of the edges curling. Dry the box slowly, evenly and thoroughly before bisque-firing to 1000°C (1832°F).

EXPERIMENTS

Once a simple box or chest has been mastered, the architecturally-inclined may want to build in great style, creating houses, castles, dream-dwellings etc., all based on this

25 Rouletted porcelain slab boxes, Simon Taylor. Made at Harrowgate College of Arts and Technology

original dolmen principle. Whatever you choose, always pay particular attention to working with slabs of the same dampness, joining seams meticulously and drying work evenly. If you need to join a thick wall to a thinner one, prevent the thin one from drying until the thick wall has caught up.

Those who are good at geometry could make octagonal boxes, or ones with two flat sides and one curved (see page 41). Experiment with abstract designs, using hexagons, rhomboids or any manner of faceted shapes (see page 43). (For creations that necessitate long narrow slabs, it is advisable to strengthen with cross-ridging to prevent warping.)

SOFT-SLABBING

Curves for beauty, angles for strength.
Bernard Leach

Soft slabs, being plastic, can be encouraged to curve into handsome shapes by being lifted into position whilst still in the material they were rolled in. They can be shaped over formers that are covered with muslin or newspaper so that the slabs won't stick and crack on drying. I have made chests with curved lids in this manner (see page 73).

Soft-slabbing is a very individual method of working clay as it can combine sculptural, painterly and vessel-like qualities in bold style. Slabbed vases can have necks and feet added as further slabs; a single sheet of clay

26 Soft-slabbed fruit bowl, Tony Birks. White earthenware glaze. Height: 30 cm (12 in.)

held in a piece of cloth can be folded into a skirt for the bottom of a pot, or collared in for the neck. Simple, quick shaping can be extremely effective and often too much handling results in the destruction of any natural tautness of the prepared slab. In fact, you can make organic sculptural forms by allowing the clay to curve, buckle or fold more or less according to its own thickness and weight. Try supporting them with crunched-up newspaper, or leave them in muslin or paper, which will burn away in the kiln. You could also leave the markings of the material where the rolling-pin has pressed. Try patterning the surface beforehand with textured material like paper doylies or machine-made lace.

Edges can be neatly squared off, chamfered, pinched into delicate shapes – only remember to dry differing thicknesses carefully and remember to use damp paper on all unfinished edges.

TIP

When cutting soft slabs before assembly, cut inwards from the edges first then across to the middle to stop the edges being distorted. Make several cuts rather than one.

CARVING, SLICING AND FACETING

Carving and slicing a pot produces strong, powerful forms that are particularly effective for raku. Study the cut raku tea-bowls made by Koetsu in eighteenth-century Japan. Bowls, jars, bottles, etc. can be faceted when leather-hard. Slice them with a sharp, long-bladed knife; make a decision, then cut precisely and firmly to produce forms with well-defined edges. Faceting must necessarily be done on a thick-walled pot. You could beat the pot roughly to shape beforehand using a wooden paddle. Leave knife-markings as evidence of how the piece was carved or plane walls smooth with a surform or gently shallow and shape the slices.

Try pushing with an eraser or blunt knife wrapped in cloth to produce a smooth, thin groove; alternatively, carve deeply to produce fat bulges that taper at both ends.

TIP

To give a well-defined ending to vertical grooving, create a foot below the pot, which will throw the grooves into relief. If the sharp arêtes between each facet are slightly rounded, then later the glaze will define them attractively by falling away neatly on either side.

CERAMIC SCULPTURE

Sculptured pieces are best made in Crank, T-Material, or clay grogged to your own specification. Sections *must* be joined thoroughly and finished work dried *very* slowly and evenly – being fired only when completely dry. Here are a few methods:

- Soft-slabbed shapes can be formed with beautiful open curves supported with balls of scrunched-up paper or damp rags left in place to burn away. Brick and cardboard make other useful supports during construction.
- Sculpture can be built up coil by coil then smoothed over – the finished areas should be kept well-covered until the whole is completed.
- Modelled sculpture can be completed, then the solid areas excavated from beneath, lest these blow up in the kiln. Or an almost-completed piece can be cut in half, excavated, then joined together again and finished.
- Enclosed volumes can be blown out to create a taut shape (see Chapter 2), then beaten to shape with a paddle.

TOOLS

Other than using your own hands, a wooden paddle will always produce strong form. At the leather-hard stage, straight or curved surform blades can be used effectively on larger sculptures. Later, work the piece

27 Detail of Proud Horse, *Julian Sainsbury, 1988. Modelled in grogged red clay using an external armature.
The pieces were cut, scraped out and re-joined, then painted with white slip and a thin oxided wash,
and fired to 1180°C and finally sanded down to age the surface. 52.5 × 52.5 cm (21 × 21 in.)*

further with a serrated kidney or length of hacksaw-blade. For a smooth finish, scrape with a flexible metal kidney, then sandpaper (wear a mask). For smaller pieces, wooden and metal spatulas or modelling tools are best. (*See* Suppliers, page 94.) For small, precisely-modelled pieces and porcelain sculpture, dental tools and small drill bits are excellent. 'Wet and dry' sandpaper can polish shapes once they have been bisque-fired.

DECORATION

Raw oxides are most effective for decoration when rubbed into the tool-markings and fired in (or sawdust-fired, Chapter 8). Work may be slipped with a white or coloured slip prior to painting – but the work must be uniformly leather-hard for application and the slip must suit the clay-body. After bisque firing, more pigment can be applied, and yet again at the glazing stage. Enamels or lustres may be added finally, or gloss and enamel paints could be used over a glazed, finished piece. Use what techniques are available to get your form to look and feel as *you* want.

Sculpture can be assembled from differently-treated bodies (*see* Chapter 12) or from differently-formed pieces re-assembled. Some of these might be rakued with brightly-coloured glazes, other parts left matt. Ceramic components could be affixed to metal, textiles, wood – anything is possible.

Dancing figure, Vanessa Pooley, 1988. 'T' Material. Height 38 cm (15 in.)

PERSONAL EXPRESSION

Expressive ceramic sculpture is so personal that only technique can be taught. There are many contemporary sculptors using clay, and it is easy to copy rather than use your own ceramic 'voice'. But going back in time I would recommend studying Gauguin, Chagall, Picasso and Miro. Excellent books are available on the ceramic work of these artists. As painters, they fuse both painterly and ceramic disciplines with great success, and their works, often finished with bright enamels and coloured glazes, are full of freshness and vitality. Further back in time, there are the wonderful T'ang figures, in which fluidity of form combine with humour and charm. Parts of these figures are moulded, with individual touches added later. Provided that you model without undercuts, your ceramic sculpture can be cast and moulded – as will be shown in the following chapter.

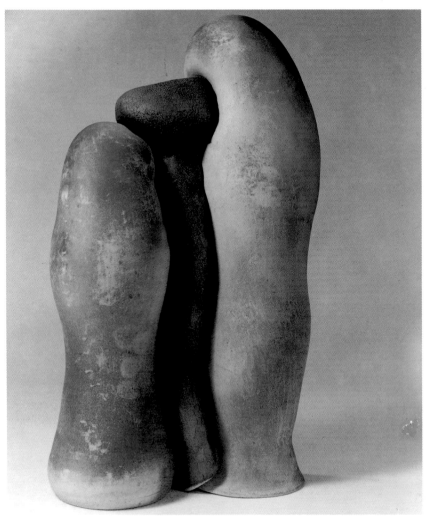

28 Untitled, Noga Wilson, 1988. Folded slabs of 'T' material with coiled areas, Raku-fired with washes of iron and copper oxides, yielding some pink and green flashes, and then smoked. Height 36.5 cm (14 in.). (Photo: Mac)

CHAPTER SEVEN

MOULDING

Plaster moulds made from your clay shapes can be used for all kinds of work. Generally, the shape that forms the model must be made from solid clay without undercuts so that it is easy to release. Bowl shapes are best, so I will give the procedure for casting one of these.

Remember that you will be modelling your bowl upside down because it is the outside silhouette that is used for a plaster cast. Include a foot-ring as long as this too has no undercuts and will lift from the mould without pulling.

The bowl should be beautifully-shaped since you will be using it to create from repeatedly. Also, it must be so perfectly smooth that it will release easily from the mould, for plaster will reveal **every single mark**. Miniscule lumps will show as hollows and miniscule hollows will appear as lumps in the cast. You can choose to throw your solid shape on the wheel, turn it on the wheel leather-hard, or model it by hand – only the last method will produce a pot that is not absolutely symmetrical. Cardboard or perspex templates are helpful if you are making an oblong or square shape.

MODELLING A ONE-PIECE DROP-OUT MOULD

MATERIALS
- rough clay for the core of your work (for casting large shapes)
- smooth clay for the top surface and supporting-walls
- round, flat, wooden batt or sheet of plate glass to work and cast on
- turn-table and modelling-tools
- turning tools
- metal kidney
- rubber kidney
- chamois leather

METHOD
Model your bowl shape upside down or on your batt or glass, leaving at least 6 cm (2¼ in) between the bowl's rim and the edge of the batt or glass, as this is where your plaster casting will go; make sure the allowance space for the plaster is completely clean and flat.

If you want to throw your shape or turn it using a slow-moving electric wheel, you must first fix your wooden batt firmly onto the wheel-head. To do this, first throw a flat clay disc on the wheel-head and make grooves in it. The wooden batt will stick to the grooved clay as you centre it. (By giving the side of the batt sharp taps while the wheel slowly turns, you should be able to centre it without too many problems.) Now press your batt down firmly and put an extra coil of clay around the underside of the batt where this touches the wheel-head, in order to secure it further.

You can make a small bowl from one lump of clay, but when making a large piece – whether turning leather-hard clay with a sharp turning tool on a slow-moving wheel, or modelling an asymmetrical form – you will need to make the core out of harder clay. Build up around this, using walnut-sized pieces of softer clay and patting these down with a wooden paddle until you reach roughly the shape you want. Compress the clay firmly as this is the foundation that will support your final working layer. Make a final layer from 5 cm (2 in) of softer, well-wedged clay. Compact this, too, so that when you turn or shave away to form the final surface, you won't discover air-pockets or uneven lumps. I use a turning tool followed by serrated kidney and finally a smooth rubber kidney to produce a smooth finish. For the last 6 mm ($\frac{1}{4}$ in) it pays to leave the clay to firm up to a leather-hard condition.

TIP

You will find it considerably easier to pare away the final fraction of clay and smooth over your completed shape with a damp chamois leather. You may even find that you have to leave the shape overnight before you can finish it to perfection. This waiting will save you hours of frustration trying to work on an uneven surface, patching it with wet clay that will not tool evenly. (Renew the supporting coil under the wheel-head if it has dried out overnight.)

CASTING A ONE-PIECE DROP-OUT MOULD

The most common casting method taught is to construct a wall around your piece, 3.5 cm ($\frac{1}{2}$ in) away from the edge and high enough to stand above the bowl's base, then fill with plaster. I never use this method because it produces heavy, uneven moulds wasteful of plaster. As plaster has to be poured level, it sets ludicrously thickly where your bowl slopes inwards towards its base. This in turn causes uneven drying for your clay casting later. Frequently, the force of the plaster breaks the clay walls, or it leaks causing further wastage and a dreadful mess. Using a piece of vinyl tied into a circle onto a clay wall is really no better. My method allows you to make a mould the exact thickness you want, spread evenly over the form you are casting, using less plaster and producing a stronger mould through the use of scrim. It is the method used to cast clay portrait heads, and can also be used to cast your ceramic sculpture.

MATERIALS
- curved 15 cm (6 in) bowl ($\frac{1}{2}$ a child's play-ball will do)
- small plastic washing-up bowl
- surform blade
- scraper
- sheet of strong polythene
- plaster of Paris or casting plaster
- scissors and some scrim (made from roughly-woven hessian), 8 cm (3 in) wide
- soft soap

METHOD

1 To cast a bowl-shape modelled upside down on a batt or glass, first place this on a turn-table. Then brush soft soap onto the exposed areas of batt or glass to stop the plaster from sticking. Pin or drape your sheet of polythene behind it to catch stray plaster. Cut enough 0.5–1 cm ($\frac{1}{4}$–$\frac{3}{8}$ in) strips of scrim to cover the model. You will need the scrim for the second layer (stage 3).

2 In the small half-ball, mix enough smooth plaster to cover the model all over to a thickness of 0.5–1 mm ($\frac{1}{2}$–$\frac{3}{8}$ in). To mix plaster smoothly sprinkle it on water until the water will no longer accept more plaster, which begins to form hills above the surface. Leave for a minute or two to allow the plaster to slake, then put your hand below the surface with your fingers outspread. Agitate firmly until the mixture turns to a creamy consistency and there are no lumps. Force all unwanted air bubbles to the surface. (You could agitate palm upwards with spread fingers when using the smaller half-ball – the object being not to break the surface and suck air-bubbles downwards.)

Holding this bowl with one hand near your model, dip the thumb and first two fingers into the liquid plaster and *flick* this onto your model from about 8 cm (3 in) away, as if you were flicking a fly off a cake – but using two fingers instead of one. Work covering the lowest part first, ending with the top, turning the turn-table when desired. The idea is to make a complete, even covering without any air-pockets trapped behind. You will soon be able to direct your flicking to place the plaster exactly where you need it, and you should be neat, making the minimum amount of mess.

Group of small moulded bowls decorated with slip-trailed inlays, Jane Waller. Average height 5–6 cm (2–2¾ in.). See page 76 for method of making

3 While the protective coat dries (approximately 15 minutes), wash the small bowl and mix a second batch of plaster in the larger bowl. While this plaster is still liquid, dip each strip of scrim into it and lay over your mould until this is covered. Pat each piece down gently. (Your clay model is safe below its hardened initial covering.) Now you have time to wash your hands again, as you can wait until the plaster is setting to the consistency of snow, before gathering it up by the handful and smoothing the whole lot over your model to an even, 2–2.5 cm ($\frac{3}{4}$–1 in) covering. You will not need to make a thicker mould as the scrim is sufficient strengthening. You could use two layers of scrim, but I have always found one sufficient – even for the hard pestling of my millefiori pieces into the mould. (*see* Chapter 11).

4 Use any extra plaster to level the top, as this will form the base of your mould and make it firm for use. You should have time to smooth your surface over before the plaster sets, as well as to wash the bowl, etc. Use the surform to finish smoothing the cast and levelling the base.

5 Once the mould has set, turn the whole thing over onto the base and knock the batt off the mould. Excavate the unwanted clay ('spoil') carefully, starting from the middle. Sometimes, you can press a piece of clay near the edge to ease it away from the mould, and pulling on this, you can lift the whole clay piece out at once. This clay spoil can be re-used as the core for your next mould.

6 Finally, neaten your mould's exterior with the surform, then remove any traces of clay from the interior with a damp sponge before allowing it to dry thoroughly for use.

Two or three-piece moulds for vases, tall bowls and sculpture can be made using this method, provided there are no undercuts. You must also divide each area to be cast separately with a 4 cm ($1\frac{1}{2}$ in) clay wall, casting a section at a time and putting small keys or 'natches' into the walls so that the finished mould-pieces lock together. It is imperative to brush plaster walls with soft soap so that they separate easily. Keep the mould-pieces joined for drying and storage to prevent warping. I use the inner tube of a bicycle tyre to hold them in place.

HUMP MOULDS

A hump mould is made by your casting the inside of a hollow plaster mould. Thus the exterior of the hump will form the interior of your future clay bowls.

First, work several layers of soft soap thoroughly into the inside of the concave mould and over the rim; work each layer well into the plaster with a sponge to ensure that the plaster hump will separate from the plaster master-mould. Now pour liquid plaster in up to the brim and let this set. Before the plaster has set, score a rough area in the centre, to which you attach a stalk for the hump mould finally to stand on. (You can also pull on the stalk to help release the mould.) Make a funnel of clay to encircle where you wish the stalk to be and seal this well so that as you pour this full of liquid plaster it will not leak. Remove the clay wall and neaten, levelling the top of the stalk.

Once the plaster has set hard, pull the hump from the master mould. You may have to soak the whole thing in warm water to help release the hump. Neaten the edge of your hump mould as this will determine the rim of your future bowls. Keep the hump mould stored inside the master mould when not in use.

PRESS-MOULDING WITH A DROP-OUT MOULD

MATERIALS
- tough clean cloth – a piece of canvas, stiff calico, or an old deck-chair cover will be suitable
- modelling-tools
- rubber kidney
- chamois-leather or soft sponge
- rolling-pin
- 1 cm ($\frac{3}{8}$ in) wooden battens for runners
- dry, clean plaster mould
- earthenware clay (best for shallow bowls and dishes as such shapes tend to warp at stoneware temperatures)

METHOD

1 Roll out a blanket of well-wedged clay on your cloth, working from the centre of the clay outwards and moving the blanket frequently so that it does not stick to the cloth. When the blanket approaches the required thickness, place your two identical wooden battens on either side to act as runners for your rolling-pin. Now you will be able to roll to produce an exact thickness of clay for your blanket.

2 Lift the rolled blanket in its cloth, resting it over your arm and hand, and flip this over into the centre of your mould with one confident movement. Trim excess clay from the edge and place the mould centrally onto a banding-wheel or slow-turning potter's wheel. With a damp sponge or rubber kidney press lightly, working spirally from the centre of your clay-blanket out to the edge. (Obviously, you cannot use the wheel with an asymmetrical mould.) When the blanket is firmly ensconced in its mould, trim the rim and neaten with a wet sponge. The rim should be completed at this stage. Finally, smooth over the whole piece with a damp chamois-leather.

3 Decorate the bowl whilst still in the mould, or leave it until it has firmed up enough to be released from the mould without distortion. Invert the bowl onto a flat board, resting the rim on a piece of polythene so that it will dry evenly and will not catch on the wood as it

shrinks inwards. Cover the outside with loose polythene.

An alternative method to making a clay blanket is to smear clay gradually into the mould, building up to the desired thickness.

PRESS-MOULDING WITH A HUMP MOULD

1 Flip your rolled-out blanket onto the centre of your hump-mould as above. Use a clean, dry piece of sheeting laid over the top to smooth the clay down well onto the mould. Start at the centre and smooth outwards. Cut the rim from the edge of the mould with a sharp scalpel-knife before neatening it with a sponge. You could also add a foot-ring at this stage, working a thin coil of clay inside the joining seam and smoothing this well in for strength.
2 When the clay has firmed up, release it from the hump and decorate it, or dry it first as above.

TIP

Do not leave your clay shape to dry for too long on the mould as it may shrink onto the hump and crack.

WORKING IN THE MOULD

THE MAGIC OF CHEESE-CLOTH OR BUTTER-MUSLIN

Here are some other methods for making pots using a mould. Many of the processes are worked using a pestle covered with cloth. The clay may stick to the inside of the mould, owing to the beating of the pestle, so stretch a damp layer of butter-muslin inside the mould first with the excess left draped over the sides. Use the excess to smooth over the inside of the pot after the pestling has finished. Also, once the completed pot is dry enough to leave the mould, you can first loosen it and then lift it out using this excess cloth.

Since I started using butter muslin I have never had a single pot left cracked and stuck in the mould. You can pestle as hard as you like: the pot can always be lifted out (*see* Chapter 11). Use the muslin also to fold over rims and press these into shape while the pot is still in the mould or after it has been taken out, but *before* peeling the cloth away. Butter-muslin imprints a texture on the outer pot's surface which is sometimes interesting to leave instead of scraping away.

BAS RELIEF

A blanket of clay makes a fine base for a sculptured plate or bowl in relief. Using some pliable, freshly-wedged clay, sculpt a raised scene of birds animals, fish, etc. Make the scene rise from the blanket, incorporating this

Torn-clay pot, Jane Waller. Made from torn earthenware clay, arranged inside a mould and covered with a silvery-black glaze. $16\frac{1}{2} \times 10$ *cm* $(6\frac{1}{2} \times 4$ *in.)*

29 Gouged out pot, Jane Waller. Made from casting slip clay, gouged and shaped in a mould. White tin glaze. 11×10 *cm* $(4\frac{1}{2} \times 4$ *in.). (Courtesy of Tony Birks)*

Oolitic bowl, Jane Waller. Stoneware wheel-scrapings pestled into a mould.
Green copper glaze painted on and sponged off the surface. 24 × 12.5 cm (9$\frac{1}{2}$ × 5 in.)

as part of the background so that your decoration does not merely 'rest' on the surface. By allowing it to emerge, the whole surface can produce a flowing form, including the rim. You can use cheese-cloth to smooth shapes over as well as press or pinch up areas, squeezing these into shape. I have sculpted a '*sea-venus*' being thrown up from the waves: the troughs and crests of the waves formed the rim and a cobalt-stained, clear stoneware glaze completed the relief.

A self-portrait or portrait of a friend is fun to do, and this is made more interesting if it fills the complete plate or bowl. Build out the features. Be creative with the hair and make the lips and eyes expressive. Use the cloth to smooth over the cheeks, indent the lips and curve the mouth – it will leave its texture behind. Carve in around the eyes and under the chin. Later, the bisqued or slip-covered surface could be painted.

TORN CLAY

Once, when I was experimenting I began to cut a slice from a large wedged rectangle of clay, but then decided to tear the rest of the slice. This left a wonderful surface in the last three inches – not dissimilar to volcanic tufa. So I constructed some volcanic pots by laying torn slices inside a vase-shaped mould, pestling them just enough to weld them together. Some of the rugged, torn shapes were left above the rim. I made a strong silvery-black glaze for them by overloading a lead glaze with 8 per cent copper oxide (*See*

colour illustration, page 54).

GOUGED-OUT POTS

Roll some white earthenware clay or casting-slip clay (*see* Chapter 10) into a blanket and leave until leather-hard. With a narrow lino-cutting tool, gouge lines across the clay in strips, pulling away the unwanted, cut-out 'worms' as this is formed. The clay being 'short' will leave behind it a serrated edge on either side of the gouge. This textured sheet can now be draped into a mould and any seams pestled together and smoothed over. Neaten the rim, dry the object and bisque-fire it. I glaze my pots with a white tin glaze (*see* fig. 29, page 54).

OOLITIC POTS

One day – when I had begun to get interested in adding colour to textured, moulded pottery – I took a plastic bowl and filled it with all the turned stoneware-scrapings from the wheel: tightly-coiled whorls of clay, jagged serrations, small peelings, worms of interlocked bands – all of which had dried to leather-hard around the wheel-head. I transported these to my plaster mould. I sprinkled a layer of these into the bottom, then sprayed water over them until; as they absorbed the moisture, they became *just* pliable. Then I gently pressed this layer down with a pestle covered with material. Gradually I added more, working up the sides of the bowl, tilting the mould so that it wouldn't all fall to the bottom. When there

were sufficient layers beaten in, I smoothed over the pestle marks with a cloth and neatened the rim.

The bowl was dried, then bisque-fired. It came out at a strange weight – again, rather like volcanic tufa rock. I brushed on a green glaze, which I then sponged off the surface so that it only filled the interstices. The glaze brought out a kind of oolitic limestone pattern, for the fossils of every tiny coil or whorl had been revealed. (Alternatively copper oxide, for example, could be rubbed into the interstices, then wiped off the surface.) I fired this bowl to 1260°C (2300°F) and found that even the sponged-off areas had been very slightly stained a pale green where the strange porous surface had absorbed a minute amount of glaze. (*See* page 55).

PORCELAIN STRAPPING

Roll out many thin, even coils of porcelain on a clean cloth. Keep these damp. Now place these in a pattern inside your mould, weaving them over one another, strapping them together. These can then be pressed down with a spotlessly-clean, cloth-covered pestle. Open coils left at the rim will break or crack, so the rim must be a strong part of the structure with all loose ends closed in – a strapped, woven or looped rim is best. You can add a foot-ring once the bowl is dry enough to lift from the mould (*see* opposite).

COMPOSITE POTS

You can build on moulded forms with coiling, always using the same batch of clay. Similarly, extend a bowl with pinching, or coiling then pinching.

30 Strapped porcelain bowl, Jane Waller. Formed in a mould. Smooth semi-opaque glaze. 19 × 10 cm (7½ × 4 in.)

CHAPTER EIGHT

Part Two: Decoration and Colour

TEXTURAL DECORATION

MAKING YOUR DECORATION WORK FOR YOU

Both texture and colour can subtly alter the structural appearance of the pot. For example, the eye will look at the complete vessel if this has an all-over pattern; otherwise, it will be drawn towards wherever the design is placed. Decorating a pot is not dissimilar to using make-up on the face. You can cleverly emphasize and even appear to alter structure. Just as the eyeshadow highlights the eye by darkening the surrounding skin, light can be made to bounce off a smooth curve and shadows can be thrown up by indentions in ceramics. A curve can be burnished, given a gloss glaze or bright colouring and it will glow and seem to hum round the pot. A series of rough, jagged cuts will create shadows, inviting secrecy and mystery. Bright colours layered together will startle and excite – like those the mountain tribesmen of southern Sudan paint on their faces to heighten the normal expression and give it greater potency.

Textural decoration should celebrate the pot's character and be conceived three-dimensionally, so that it is well-balanced and appropriate to the form. It should suit the pot in scale as well as in relationship to itself. Fortunately, by its very nature, textural decoration can become part of the pot's body rather than an added 'finish'.

In its raw state, clay can be patterned and textured in a variety of ways from its soft stage to totally hard as described below.

CLAY STATE

METHODS OF PATTERNING	
Soft	Squeezing, cloth-moulding, marbling, feathering, slip-trailing and pouring over textured surfaces.
Pliable	Moulding with the hands i.e. – pinching, coiling, squeezing and pulling. Extruding, impressing, combing with a wooden comb, embossing and making prunts and sprigs, intrusions of other clay.
Leather-hard	Etching, carving, incising, cutting, luting, roughening, smoothing, burnishing, inlaying, scraping, painting. Combing with a metal comb.
Beyond leather-hard	Scratching, burnishing, scraping with a metal kidney, working with kitchen scourer, painting.
Bone-hard	Sand-papering, painting. Working on porcelain.

PRESSING

SOFT CLAY

Gentle

You can make gentle markings on damp clay by wrapping textured cloth around the pot and pressing the design through. This can be anything from delicate lace, through textured furnishing fabrics and woven textiles, to rough scrim or floor-cloth. Similarly, paper could be used, from patterned paper doylies, through textured wallpapers, to corrugated cardboard. As well as the usual leaf, twig, bone, or reed, experiment by using a rush woven table-mat or roll your pot on the coconut matting. Maybe you could use crochet, knitting, embroidery – a cat's cradle made from string?

Strong

For a more dramatic effect, wrap some string around your damp pot – you could use a cat's cradle here, too – and pull the pot's shape in. (Try doing this with a 'blown-up' pot, Chapter 2.) Or try throttling your pot's neck with tightly-wound knitting yarn or a piece of patterned cotton crochet. The clay will fold, wrinkle and look quite unusual.

You could dimple a damp pinch pot or thin-walled coil pot by pressing the cloth-covered point of a ball pen gradually until a depression is formed on, say, three or four evenly-spaced positions round the pot's widest point. This will leave behind the dimpled effect made from the pulled-in surrounding walls.

LEATHER-HARD CLAY

When your pot is slightly harder, textured materials can be wrapped around a paddle and slapped against a pot. (Remember that although you are decorating, you are still forming, so your actions must be directed accordingly.) You can also use this method on a 'blown-up' pot before the clay plug is taken out; the pot will retain its shape as you beat it because of the air trapped inside.

Cord or string was used by the prehistoric Japanese Jōman potters to press into or roll over the pot's surface (*Jō-mon* means 'cord pattern'). Close tightly-touching bands were wound with knotted cord to produce handsome and individual designs. Additional texture was created by adding shells or rouletting with carved sticks. Some areas, already deeply-incised, had slashed, notched ridges added, or were embossed with ribbons of textured clay. Rims were exuberantly carved and ridged with sculptured asymmetrical designs (*see* fig. 7, page 13).

Try winding string in well-grouped bands of differing dimension to produce smart, subtle decoration. (The string will burn off in the kiln.) If the string is positioned thoughtfully, this can directly alter your pot's proportions, for it will determine where the eye will rest.

The African potters use sticks to impress patterns that echo those of their baskets, woven cloth or body markings. Some of these patterns contrast with the smoothly-burnished areas in between. If a coil-pot is fashioned inside a basket for a mould, as it is in Ghana, then a pattern is instantly obtained.

An unlimited range of found objects can be requisitioned from around the house for decorating. Starting in the kitchen, you could come away with the cheese-grater, apple-corer or a fork. (I often use a wooden pastry-wheel or 'roulette', which leaves behind it a crisp, wavy line.) From the bathroom make use of that old toothbrush, comb or bent wriggly hair-pin; raid the sewing-box for a thimble, knitting-needle or buttons. The garage yields ingenious things to push into a pot – nuts, bolts, nails, surforms, files or pieces of hacksaw blade. If none of these items are to hand, you could just use the impression from a ring or other jewellery – even your finger-nail can be employed to make crosses and diagonal lines.

A trip to the seaside will provide shells, sea-etched driftwood, dried seaweed, as well as smoothed pebbles for burnishing.

Like the patterns seen through a kaleidoscope, you could make a pleasing pattern using multiple pressings from any of the articles above – whether formed into a circle, diamonds, zig-zags, triangles, oblongs or flowers. Use a pattern off your Guernsey knitwear or the kelim carpet for inspiration. Grouping patterns together is far more pleasing than indiscriminately pressing into the pot's surface.

OTHER METHODS OF DECORATING

EMBOSSED DESIGN

Rosettes, medallions, prunts and pressings make imposing decorations, particularly on slab- or bottle-pots where a flat area may provide a place of interest. On curved pots decoration should harmonize with the silhouette, so take care that it makes an important addition rather than blemish the surface. (The German Bellarmine jars exemplify well-placed, embossed design.) You can make you own stamps by carving a design in wood or clay; either bisque-fire the clay before use, or, after making a 4 cm (1½ in) wall of clay around it, cast the design in plaster or cellulose filler. Press runic script or hieroglyphics into prunts and then apply them to the pot's surface for a mysterious effect. Either support the wall from the inside as you stick or tap on your stamped impression, or just leave the dimpled area caused by the pulled-in surrounding clay wall.

INCISING

Incising is an embellishment found on some of the oldest pots in existence. On the burnished, thin-walled Neolithic pottery of the Nile, (which the Nubian potters fashioned from Nile silt tempered with cattle-dung), fishbone skeletons were used to incise fine, triangular motifs, derived from basketware patterns. The Nubians then filled the incising with white chalk to reveal the design.

31 Coil pot krater with flowers in relief, from the Palace of Phaistos, Crete, 2000–1700 BC. (Courtesy of the Heraklion Museum)

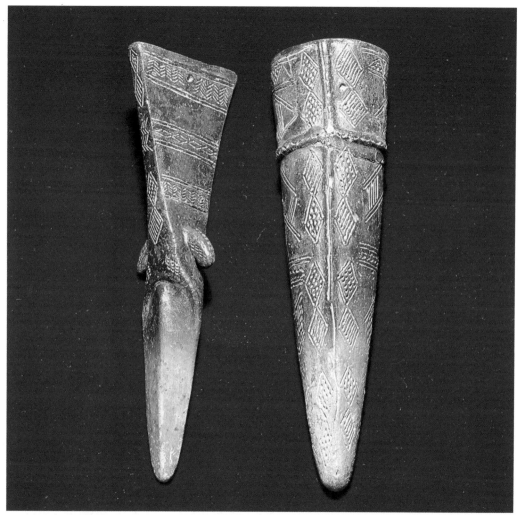

Incising is especially admirable on coil pots, where it forms an intrinsic part of the wall. Parallel combed lines, circles and geometric markings made with a wood or metal comb can emphasize the fullness of a pot if placed round its widest point – or just below and above this. Alternatively, incising can embellish a vessel's neck and base. Make bold designs on large pots, or neat, intricate

Clay knife and sheath, Cyprus, Early Bronze Age. Black-topped, red polished ware, with incised decoration. Knife length: 21 cm (8 in.). Sheath length: 21.5 cm (8¼ in.). (Photo: Desmond Morris; courtesy of the Desmond Morris Collection)

designs, on medium or small ones, using the
same scoring implements as those used in
ancient times: sticks, pips, bones, bamboo,
shells or stones. Modern day bevelling-tools
or a lino-cutting set can give a variety of
grooves, and a length of hack-saw blade or
serrated metal kidney makes dynamic
sweeping circles and rhythmic markings.

CARVING

African potters often intentionally coil thicker
walls, so that they can carve deeply into the
surface to make designs as strong as those of
their wood-carving. Often, these carvings are
accompanied by more delicate pressing from
lightly-textured knotted cord on flat areas in
between. (Be careful not to dig too deep when
carving or the walls may crack.)

   Shallow carving on bone hard or low-
bisqued porcelain looks beautiful on thin
walls where translucency allows light to glow
gently. Walls can be pierced half way or
completely – but this is painstaking work and
requires a great amount of patience and skill
(*see* Chapter 4).

FLUTING AND RIBBING

A fluting tool has a tautly-looped wire that is
drawn through the clay. Fluting is used
effectively on a slabbed or carved pot, since
the furrows, being cut, echo the way the pot
itself was made. Curved, shallow fluting on a
fine-bodied clay pot looks graceful; used
deeply-grooved on a grogged pot, they look
strong. Experiment with different fluting

*32 Bowl, Jane Perriman, Coiled 'T' material,
covered with slips and smoked. 23 × 17 cm
(9 × 6½ in.)*

tools, making narrow, broad, curved, spiral,
straight or triangular grooves. If the pot is
carinated with a shelf above and below the
grooves, then this will throw their edges into
relief. Neat, tight, horizontal ribbing around
the base of the pot can help create a shadow
to lift the shape of the pot above.

Three mystical figures, Anne Marie Turner. Red earthenware, painted slips (smoked). 44 cm (17 in.)

REDUCTION FIRING

BURNISHING

Burnishing a coil pot creates a tight surface (*see* page 37). Red earthenware clay is best to use as burnish will not fire away at low temperatures. By pressing a burnishing-pebble slightly into the surface of a pot just beyond leather-hard, and rubbing round and round, clay molecules are compressed and made to lie flat. The pot is thereby strengthened and the surface made more impervious. Try burnishing your pots, using the back of a desert spoon or pebble. Work on one area at a time until completely smooth. Alternatively, burnish along the lines of the pot and leave directional press-markings. Diagonal burnishing, worked from base to rim, also leaves attractive spiral markings as a subtle decoration.

Burnishing adds colour to the pot when an *engobe* or slip containing oxides is rubbed in to colour the body. Both the Nile and the Mimbres potters, for example, engobed their pots with red haematite, which they mixed with water into a creamy slip and burnished once this had lost its tackiness. In India and Iran a lump of haemetite itself is used to rub onto the surface.

Burnished pots are beautiful when given an oxidized firing to 1000°C (1832°F). They remain red, and when subsequently polished, glow with a surface as smooth as a chestnut or polished wood. Pots are also beautiful when heavily-reduced in a sawdust-firing, so that carbon deposits cast areas of colour that range from a matt, smokey grey to a deep carbonaceous black (*see* fig. 32, page 62). Smooth areas will blacken more intensely than roughened areas.

SAWDUST REDUCTION FIRING

'Reduction' is the process whereby the kiln fuel is deprived of oxygen so that it combines with the oxides inside the clay (see colour illustration, page 63). This blackens the surface of the clay, which when polished takes on a dull, gun-metal sheen. Gabrielle Koch's pots are treated this way.

To achieve this effect put a layer of sawdust into a saggar – a box made from fire-clay (*see* tip). Place your pot inside this, then fill the saggar with sawdust. Fit on the lid and fire from 700 to 900°C (1292 to 1652°F) in a gas or solid-fuel kiln – never in an electric one. If the smouldering sawdust produces a streaky pot, you can re-fire or even re-oxidize in a normal kiln. Bisque-firing your pots first in an oxidizing kiln will make them stronger, but this generally produces areas that are grey or pinkish, whereas raw clay will turn really black.

In 750–80 AD, when the Mimbres tribe changed from producing red ware to greyish-black ware, it is intriguing to conjecture that they did so by stumbling across the reduction process. If a flue had accidently become blocked the atmosphere in the kiln would have reduced and blackened the clay within. This may have delighted them so much, that they consequently reduced all their pots.

TIP

A new way of smoking ceramic forms in an electric kiln without using a saggar is to use tin foil. According to how much reduction you require, wrap strips of newspaper around your piece (fewer strips = less reduction). Then enclose the pot completely in the foil, leaving some air inside between the foil layer and pot, and fire it to 450°C (842°F) for about three hours. Anne Marie Turner produced a light reduction on her piece (page 63) by wrapping 5 cm (2 in) strips around the top and the bottom. Glazed areas resisted the smoke (See page 63).

Before glazing was developed, burnishing was obviously the best available method of making an earthenware pot less porous, smoother and easier to clean. The surface may also have been greased and, to protect the contents within, the pot finally sealed with a lid made from a cone of mud.

Africans are the undoubted geniuses of burnishing, and an excellent place to see some examples is in the Museum of Mankind, London.

CHAPTER NINE

PAINTING ON POTTERY

PAINTED DESIGN

In pottery painting, the frame is provided by the shape of the vessel, whose three-dimensional contours are at once a handicap and an opportunity, giving scope for invention of pattern which must always be in harmony or effective contrast with the 'movement' of the vessel's form.

W.B. Honey, *The Art of the Modern Potter*,
1944

Design must follow the pot's rhythm and form. A splendidly-made pot can easily be ruined by a hesitant, niggling decoration. I suggest two rules:

1 THINK IN CURVES

Have the whole of your pattern in mind when decorating a part of it. Imagine that you are decorating the volume of air inside the pot. In this way you will be made aware of its three-dimensional character. Practise painting on a jam-jar, you will see how what you are painting relates to the rest of the design. Better still, paint on a glass sphere; then your

vision will encompass top and bottom as well as around.

Look at the curves of the Minoan pots from Phaistos (*see* page 8); Jennifer Aamon's coil pot (page 33); or the Neolithic pot from China (page 17).

33 Left: *Zuni pot, from the Mesa Verde.* Right: *Mimbres black and white geometric pot.* (Courtesy of the trustees of the British Museum)

2 NO NEGATIVE SPACE

The space around your decoration is as important as the decoration; be aware of the areas you are NOT painting. Once again the Mimbres potters demonstrate this. For sheer geometric elegance, their decoration is still unrivalled (*see* fig. 33, page 65). Whether simple or complex, abstract or representational, the design always 'fills' the bowl. This is done by the superb balancing of the positive and negative forms; thus, like the yin and yang symbol, sometimes the black shape dominates, sometimes the white. There is no 'extra' space in between. The only instance in the Mimbres pottery when the pattern dominates its surrounding space is if a human or animal form is depicted, when the emotional context denotes greater importance (*see Further reading.*)

USING SYMBOLS AS DECORATIONS

Such was the imagination of the Mimbres people, that in the 150 years of their black and white period, over 7,000 designs were produced. Many of these were stylized symbols steeped in mythology, which went back thousands of years and were shared universally by many civilizations. Representations of lightning zig-zags or clouds or rain used by the Pueblo and Hopi Indians, are still used on our weather-maps today; those for mountains and wavy water-lines are used on our traffic signs. In ancient times they were magically invested with the power of invocation or myth, similar to Egyptian or Greek ceramics.

Considered sacred, Pueblo pottery was particularly infused with such lore. Powerfully-painted symbols of stylized animals, enclosures, rain-gods and people, were formed into strong geometric patterning like those on their textiles and baskets. Sometimes the insides of the animals were depicted – like the digestive tract and the uterus – probably to ensure that the animals would be living and able to eat and reproduce in the next world (*see* page 2). Although women made the pots, the ceremonial pieces were often decorated by the men and used in ceremonies performed by men. Because the Spanish church authorities eventually forbade the Pueblos to bury vessels with their dead, few examples have been handed down.

Today's new language of symbols tends to derive from the mixture of cultures and the diversity of popular imagery that surrounds us. It is usually intellectually rather than spiritually derived, reflecting our way of life, although sometimes the mystical or metaphysical is evident. Siddig El Nigumi, for example, has decorated his sgraffito bowls with modern traffic-flow arrows on signs or anti-nuclear symbols; yet the borders of his bowl are of Sudanese origin. The combination imparts a mystical quality to both (*see* fig. 34 opposite). Liz Fritsch, makes pots about music and covers them with an engobe, a slip which is then painted with subtle colouring and fired unglazed to retain the soft appearance of a fresco (*see* colour illustration opposite). Musical notations of colour are translated into patterns which move on the static pot's surface so that this is dissolved and the eye tricked spacially into a metaphysical state of rhythm and paradiddle.

You will find it helpful to look at some ancient examples of symbolism as a starting-point. Then look around you and find symbols which you think say something about contemporary life. You can just represent abstract geometric designs which have no significance beyond a pattern. Often the key to a successful piece is in the simplicity of design.

OXIDES

The oxides that we use to paint and colour ceramics are geologically-derived metallic oxides occurring naturally in rock structures. Oxides change depending upon whether they are high or low-fired, oxidized or reduced, mixed together or used in conjunction with manufactured stains. They can be used in a strength varying from 1 to 10 per cent – though strong oxides like the coppers, cobalts, chrome or vanadium, need to be used very sparingly – no more than 2 to 3 per cent, or they will bloat, unless an overloaded effect is desired. You can paint designs using underglaze body stains or oxides onto either greenware or bisqued pots before glazing.

34 Greenham Common, *Siddig El' Nigoumi,*
1985. Decorated by sgraffito through black
and red slip. 23 × 23 cm (9 × 9 in.)

Jazz piano duo, Elizabeth Fritsch, 1987.
Stoneware painted with slip. This was one of
the ceramic designs for the British
commemorative stamps issued in 1988

(Check which oxides will disappear at stoneware temperatures and use them only on earthenware.)

Because oxides are powdery, it is a good idea to add a little gum arabic (tragacanth) to give a thicker consistency to work with. Otherwise, load your brush generously, as did the potters from Phaistos, Crete, and make designs with bold, self-confident brushstrokes. A fine spraying of gum arabic over this will set the design.

Many of today's large jug and vase shapes from soft-slabbed clay make excellent canvases for painted designs beneath a transparent glaze. Bruce McClean's painterly treatment of large slipped pieces or John Maltby's decorated enamel slab-formed pieces are expressions of optimism and joy. Henry Pim uses glaze, then slip-trails or flicks slip with a brush on top of glaze, building up layers of decoration in multiple firings. Confidence and a sweepingly-applied brush will bring good rewards, according to skill. You have to be gifted to decorate your piece with only one or two wonderful brush-strokes of coloured slip or oxide, like those found on the handsome, stylized Cufic writing of an early cream-slipped Samarkand dish. But economy of line is effective, as can be seen from the brush of a Chinese, Korean or Egyptian Master (*see* fig. 12, page 18).

If a piece of ceramic is first slip-covered, this makes an excellent vehicle for decoration, and has a wider firing-range than most glazes (*see* Chapter 12).

35 Slab-built pot in buff stoneware, Henry Pim, 1982. Decorated with glaze and then slip applied on top of glaze by a brush and a slip trailer. Multi-fired to 1260°C (2300°F). Height 46 cm (18 in.)

CHAPTER TEN

SLIPS

A BASE FOR PAINTING

Using slips as a paint base for pottery is similar to using gesso as preparation for painting on wood or a coat of primer before painting on canvas. A cool, white-slipped bowl or plate makes a tempting surface for decoration, giving extra vitality to the design painted over it. Kenzan discovered that even black had more vibrancy and depth if painted over white slip. A transparent or semi-transparent glaze is normally used over slip work to reveal colours and any subsequently painted design. Finally, enamels or lustre can be added during a third, lower firing.

Slip is a mixture of clay and colouring oxides diluted to a creamy consistency with water. Some secondary clay such as ball clay is added to assist plasticity while reducing shrinkage. Use it well-mixed after passing it through an 80–100 mesh sieve. Slip can be sprayed, dipped or brushed onto dry or leather-hard clay before bisque-firing, or prior to burnishing or painting. It should be composed of the same clay as the body it is to join. However, in the case of finding a *white*

slip to cover a stoneware or red earthenware, it is a matter for experiment. Not being composed of the same clay, the slip will often peel or crack before or during firing. Here are three recipes for white slips:

1 Up to cone 10 (*Leach*): 60 china clay, 20 ball clay, 20 feldspar. (This can be used on bisqued ware).

2 Cone 4–9 (*Shaffer*): 25 china clay; 25 ball clay; 10 feldspar; 25 flint; 10 talc; 5 borax.

3 Cone 6–11 (*Shaffer*): 23 china clay; 22 ball clay; 20 feldspar; 30 flint; 5 borax.

COLOURED SLIP

A basic cream slip (see below) mixed with different metallic oxides produces a wide variety of colours. Experiment with your own. Here are a few dark shades so that paler tones can be made by decreasing the proportion of oxide: for a pale green, for example, add only 1 per cent copper carbonate.

Basic cream: 55 ball clay; 45 china clay; 4 iron oxide; 2 rutile.

Dark green: 6 copper carbonate; 1 nickel oxide.
Brown: 5 iron oxide; 5 manganese dioxide.
Beige: 4 iron oxide; 4 manganese dioxide.
Pink: 6 red iron oxide.
Blue: 2 cobalt oxide; 2 manganese dioxide. Or alternatively: 2 red iron oxide; 1 cobalt oxide.
Grey/blue:1–2 cobalt carbonate; 2–3 red iron oxide.
Black: 2 cobalt oxide; 6 manganese dioxide; 2 copper oxide. Or alternatively: 15 per cent of iron oxide; 3 per cent of either cobalt oxide or manganese dioxide.

(If slip is to be used over a red earthenware body, 5 per cent cobalt oxide added to dry red clay will make black, while 1 per cent manganese dioxide will give dark brown.)

Try painting with just black on white or red on white, as this can be particularly effective. A banding-wheel will facilitate making bands of colour or borders and is also helpful for repetitive patterns. While turning the wheel with one hand, you can be decorating with the other.

DIPPING

For dipping, slip should be fairly liquid and very well sieved. Dunk the vessel with quick, confident movements into the slip and immediately out again. The covering should be evenly applied, and with a small shake of the wrist you can get rid of drips.

If a bowl is first given a complete coating of slip, and a coloured slip is trailed onto the still-wet surface, the slips will merge. Two such methods are:

MARBLING

One slip is poured into the bowl while in the mould, then poured out. Now a second slip is poured in immediately and the mould tilted, tipped and moved round smartly to confuse the two slips, producing a marbled effect.

Try different colours together. Try moving the mould with different swirling movements to see how the pattern is altered.

FEATHERING

A foundation layer of slip is poured into a shallow dish in its mould, and before this has lost its dampness, lines of another colour are trailed in thick, liquid, close lines across the dish. While this is still wet, a feather is drawn deftly but delicately through the trails at right angles, drawing one line of colour into the next.

Experiment with drawing different instruments through the slips in sweeping movements. Maybe using a metal comb, or a tuft cut from a broom?

36 Cave drawings, Siddig El' Nigoumi, 1985. Diameter 35 cm (14 in.)

OTHER DECORATIVE EFFECTS

SLIP-TRAILING

A slip-trailer is a rubber bulb with nozzle, available from all pottery stockists. To ensure an even flow from the trailer, the slip should be thoroughly mixed and sieved before use; any lumps will block the nozzle. However, as a slightly stiffer mix of slip is needed for slip-trailing, a little gum arabic can be added to improve the flow and adhesion so that the line will not dribble out of shape.

Load the bulb with slip, and with practise and confidence, flowing lines, curves, rhythmic patterns or spots and other small motifs can be trailed onto a leather-hard pot. Henry Pim uses glaze, then slip-trails or flicks slip with a brush on top of glaze, building up layers of decoration in multiple firings.

If you are new to slip-trailing, practise first on newspaper, for hesitation will show. Before long you will be able to make pointillé pictures or neat cross-hatched borders on your pottery. When not in use, the slip should be kept in an air-tight, lidded, plastic bucket, and the slip-trailer emptied then washed clean.

LETTERING

Lettering a plate or dish with a slip-trailer over either the natural clay or a slipped coating can make unusual decoration. A portrait plate with written dedication round the rim will make a fine present for an anniversary, christening or memorial because it will have the quality of the personal and unique. The intimate slip-ware of Thomas Toft, the seventeenth-century Staffordshire potter, should be studied for its charm and confidence.

SLIP ON SLIP

Dramatic pictures or patterning can be trailed using contrasting coloured slips. First cover your pot with a coating of, say, a dark blue, brown or green slip, then trail a design in white slip over this. A stark black slip can be trailed over a white- or cream-dipped bowl in coils, diamonds or loops. Maybe you could

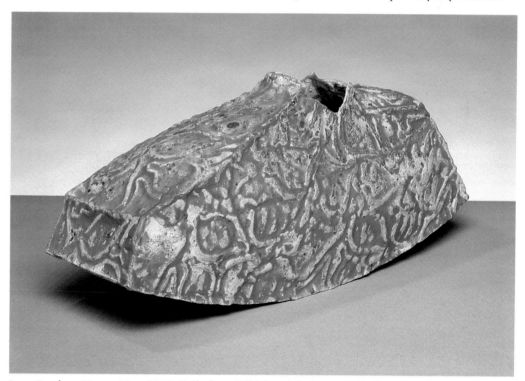

Low Rocker, Henry Pim, 1987. Built from 'T' Material. 16 cm (6¼ in.)

apply slip with different implements like crinkled cloth, cotton wool or a feather?

SPRIGGING

Josiah Wedgwood is most readily associated with sprigging. His figures, made from white-slipped designs formed in shallowly-carved plaster moulds, were pasted with slurry onto the shoulders of his cold, Attic-blue vases. Personally I find them too cold and formal. How about some experiments?

With your slip-trailer, extrude a piece of close, tight pattern in a colour slip thickened with gum arabic onto a plaster batt. While this is still flexible, place it carefully onto a pot you have just slipped in another colour and which is the correct dampness to accept your design. Your pattern can be lifted off the plaster batt with a wide, flat, metal spatula then pressed on carefully with your hands. Sprigging must be worked fairly quickly before your pattern has a chance to dry out and become too brittle to handle, but you can dampen your plaster batt slightly to cause a delay. Try a repeated trailed motif to encircle the pot's shoulder, lifting or tipping your design onto a cloth first to facilitate wrapping it onto the vase – or roll the pot lightly over the design so that its coating of damp slip will pick this up. The pot might be first slipped with a coloured band the dimension of the design, so that it becomes a frieze. If your added design is an open one, you may want to infill some of the latticed areas with a further colour, using the slip-trailer. This will

look rather like cloisonné enamel.

ICING MACHINES

I have used icing-machines and most of the nozzles to produce a variety of prunts, stars, squiggles, etc. using coloured slips. The slips should be thick and well-mixed (try adding a little vinegar as a thickener). Keep the nozzle-ends you are not using in a damp cloth so that slip doesn't harden in the spout. (One thing to remember, is not to leave prunts with sharp points. These will cause unpleasant burrs even when covered with glaze. But you could try gently patting the design into the pot's surface when this has dried to leather-hard, or even burnish it in.)

BURNISHING SLIP

If slip decoration is put onto a vessel already coated with slightly drier slip, and both are left to dry to leather-hard, they can then be burnished. Fiona Salazar's pieces are made in this way. She uses a special *terra sigillata* mix of slip on her elegant forms (*see* opposite).

INLAID SLIP

Coloured slip can be inlaid into most of the surface textures discussed in Chapter eight. Slip shrinks as it dries, so the impressions must be well-filled. It doesn't matter if this causes spillage and mess because once the slip has dried hard as the surrounding clay, you only have to scrape the surface with a metal kidney to reveal a crisp, sharp pattern beneath.

SLABBING WITH PATTERN INLAY

Slabs can be inlaid with patterns before being used to make boxes or chests, etc. I make ceramic treasure-chests (see page 88) by inlaying both slip-filled patterns and millefiori pieces into slabs of grogged clay. I use metal printing-punches to make extra border patterns, and a pastry-wheel to form wavy lines. I fill all interstices with coloured slips, to which I add 10 per cent molochite powder to reduce shrinkage – though you do not have to do this if the indentations are small. A V-shaped luting tool will form a groove which will hold inlaid slip better than a curved shallow groove, though these, too, will hold well after a little burnishing with the back of a spoon.

When the walls are dried to a good leather-hard texture, the chest is assembled. Then the whole piece is scraped with a pliable metal kidney to reveal a clean-edged inlay, looking a little like marquetry. I usually glaze my chests with a matt transparent glaze (Chapter 12), then sand-blast the surface. The glaze reveals the colour, but the sand-blasting ages the surface, giving it a dense, silky texture, like a sea-smoothed pebble.

IMPRESSED SLIP

Robert Cooper takes impressions off textured material by casting them in stained slips. He then assembles these coloured slabs into a pot or mural, maybe rakuing or smoke-firing some of the pieces beforehand (*see* page 74).

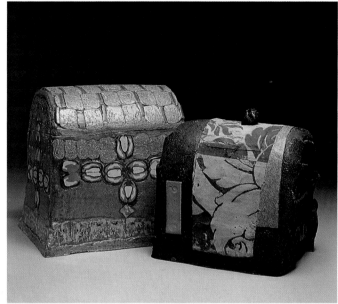

Treasure chests, (left) Jane Waller, (right) Robert Cooper, both 1987. (Left) millefiori pieces and coloured slip inlaid into heavily-grogged earthenware, then glazed, sand-blasted and refired using enamels. (Right) textured and impressed stoneware, with slipped mould pieces, using mould of fabric as a basis and glazed with transfers and enamels.

Lemon and black pot, Fiona Salazar, 1988. Coiled, low-fired earthenware, painted with terra sigilata slip using oxides and body stains, then burnished. Height 35 cm (14 in.)

SGRAFFITO

Incising makes a mark straight into the pot's wall: sgraffito scratches a design through one layer of slip to reveal the darker or lighter body of the clay below. This forms very attractive decoration. Sharp thin-bladed, round- or straight-ended instruments can be used. A keen-edged luting-tool can be used to excavate larger unwanted areas.

Siddig El' Nigoumi burnishes his bowls first, then paints on a coat of slip which he reburnishes. The design is scratched through this top coating with a steel knitting needle. Siddig uses a batten of wood rested across the mould to steady his hand. Sometimes he adds a little oxide to his transparent glaze to colour the design gently (*see* page 70).

LAYERED SLIP

After dipping a dish with several layers of black and white or coloured slips, allow the pot to dry to just before leather-hard. Now you can carve, pierce or lute with *VERY* sharp tools through all or just some of the landscapes. Thus you could expose various strata, making your own eroded sands. Alternating layers of different thickness could be dipped. You might be tempted to enlarge your depth of field still further by adding coloured sprigging and carving through the various layers between. (This method might also be worked with laminated coloured clays.)

37 Knobbly pot, Robert Cooper. Textured and impressed stoneware, with slabbed moulded pieces, using moulds of fabric as a basis, and glazed with transfers and enamels.

EXPERIMENTING WITH CASTING SLIP

CASTING SLIP

Ordinary clay slip for decorating contains 60 per cent water. With casting slip poured into plaster moulds, the addition of soda ash and sodium silicate as a deflocculant weakens the bonds between particles and reduces the water content to 40–45 per cent, while the plasticity of the slip remains. (Deflocculants cause clay to have liquid properties with only little added water.) Casting slip is usually only available in schools and colleges where there are blungers (machines with paddles that work like concrete mixers, keeping the clay from settling and forming a skin). In these the slip can be properly mixed to the correct pint weight, but it **can** be bought ready-mixed. Casting slip is bisqued to 1140°C (2084°F) and glazed at earthenware temperatures.

SLIP-COVERED CLOTH

Cloth can be dipped into casting-slip and formed into shapes inside a mould. When these are fired later, the cloth burns away, leaving a delicate shell of clay, which can then be sprayed with oxides and glaze. I find this an exciting method, and have used coloured casting slips and sometimes slip-trailed designs inside crinkled, folded or frilled shapes. Cloth formations do not necessarily have to be vessel-shaped.

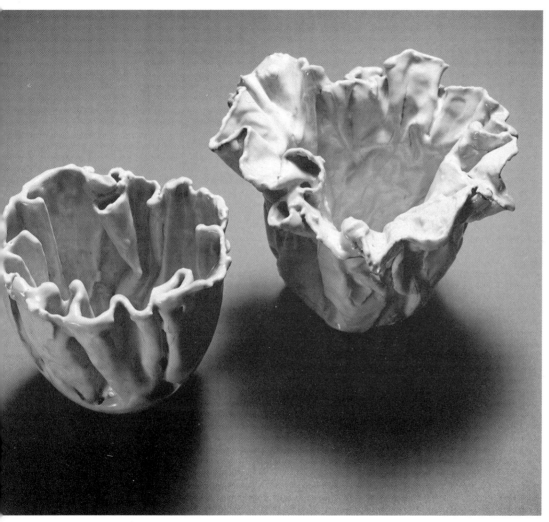

MOULDED COLOUR INLAY

I like to think that I invented this method in the early seventies. I certainly never met anyone else doing it at that time. In effect, it is decorating the mould first, then forming the pot behind the decoration. When casting slip is poured onto the decoration inside a mould and sets, it pulls the pattern away from the mould's surface, embedding it in its own. The design has to be worked out in advance as you are working against time – though the mould can be dampened slightly to retard the pattern's drying.

As it is the outside of the pot that receives the inlayed design, tall-sided vases can be worked, provided you can reach inside to make your initial decoration with the slip-trailers.

For this method you will need some rubber bulbs of coloured slip to make your design; a bowl of coloured casting-slip to form a background behind this pattern; and a bowl of plain casting slip that will become your pot's body. (You could use ordinary slips for each layer but you must use the same clay body, so that they shrink at the same rate.)

38 Slip-covered cloth is put in a mould and then fired. The cloth burns away leaving delicately fluted shapes. (Jane Waller)

First, with your slip-trailers, working deftly, decorate inside your plaster mould. Try to make the design connect with itself so that any 'ends' will not dry too fast and fall to the bottom of the mould. Alternatively, make small geometric patterns like dashes, dots, crosses etc. so that you can have the whole bowl decorated before the design dries and falls. You can lightly mist-spray the mould first with water – or the slip pattern itself, being careful not to let it run – though be aware that a wet mould will cause subsequent layers of slip to take longer to dry.

Next, *very carefully*, pour some of the background slip into the bowl, tipping it round to cover your design and the whole of the bowl's inside. Or, if you don't want pouring-marks, fill the whole bowl with the coloured slip, topping it up so that a mark isn't left on the sides when the level drops, owing to water from the clay being absorbed by the plaster walls. (This pouring *MUST* be done while your design is still well-stuck onto the walls and not dried out.) Let this layer be quite thick. Tip out excess.

Leave until dry enough to press a rubber kidney lightly over the surface to ensure you have picked up all the inlay; then fill the mould with the plain casting-slip, pouring out the excess after the desired bowl-thickness is reached.

After this layer has dried to just leather-hard, neaten and finish the rim, then pour in a layer of the background slip to colour the bowl's inside.

When the bowl has dried enough to enable you to release it from the mould, you will find that your trailed slipped design has now been inlaid into the outside of your coloured bowl. If one or two bits of your design have not adhered, it is easy enough to press them gently into place before the pot's surface has dried completely!

TIP

Because I often had to dampen the mould to allow myself time to finish before the design dried, the casting slip would takes ages to set. I found that by mixing a little fine silver-sand to the slip that the design stuck better. So I put some sand into the backing colour, too, and this stuck well. The sand softened the colours in a pleasing way.

This method would be lovely using porcelain slip. By keeping the layers fine, the pattern would become a shadowed design surrounded by translucency.

CHAPTER ELEVEN

COLOURED CLAY

INLAY

For many years I have experimented with building layers of colour and pattern within the clay body, achieved by staining or inlay. This allows me to combine construction, decoration and form. No longer do I think, '*I have made the pot, now how shall I decorate it?*'

If you are interested in staining clay, make your own test pieces; gradually build up a palette and record information as you proceed. I never use more than 5 per cent of any one oxide, but I seldom mix an oxide colour neat: I usually use a combination of two or more. I also keep necklaces of coloured clay-beads and oblong test-pieces for reference, which I string across my work-space.

Picture inlay, Jane Waller. Coloured stoneware clays and silver-sand moulded in cloth within a mould and fired unglazed to 1080°C (1976°F)

COLOURED PICTURE INLAY

I thought it would be interesting to make designs from torn, rolled, cut strips, petals or other shaped pieces of assorted coloured clay. These, like pieces of coloured felt, would be inlaid into a blanket of clay already positioned in the mould. At first I did this using coloured stoneware pieces that ranged from a hard to soft consistency, according to the amount that I wanted each piece to spread and stretch. These were inlaid into a design using a cloth-wrapped pestle.

For high-sided bowls, this was not entirely satisfactory as only the inside could be patterned; so I decided to decorate a plaster slab with the design and roll a blanket of clay over it. This was creating the decoration first – the same idea as the slip-trailed method in the previous chapter.

I use two plaster slabs: one dry on which I roll and shape the stained clay pieces; the second damp, where these pieces are transferred to be composed for the finished design. Next, I press a clay backing blanket of even thickness on top, then roll it with a rolling-pin to inlay the design. I lift the completed blanket carefully from the plaster slab and ease it design-side down into the mould. Then gently press it into place and smooth using a piece of cloth.

The method worked elegantly for me: the pieces were well-spread and neat-edged, and it was agreeable to have some of the design cut off where the rim was later trimmed. The pattern had become spread further than I

anticipated.

Liking this spreading action, I decided to expand the pattern further once it was placed in the mould, so I lightly compressed the blanket with the pestle. Again the design was stretched so that it ran over the rim in unexpected places. I inlaid further patterning, pestling it into the bowl's inside.

HUMP MOULD DECORATION AND SAND PICTURES

When I wrapped a designed blanket of pattern, formed as above, over a hump mould, and rolled it on using a small lino-inking roller, I found that sometimes pieces of my pattern would remain behind. They annoyingly stuck to the hump and sometimes onto the plaster slab to begin with, so finally, I sprinkled some silver-sand onto the damp-plaster bat before decorating it. The sand stopped the blanket sticking to the slab and also strengthened the pot; it prevented shrinkage, cracking and warping, producing a pleasingly-textured surface once I had fired my pieces unglazed to stoneware maturing point. The oxide colours, too, had gently softened in tone behind the sand (*see* colour illustration, page 77).

Since working on these last two methods, I discovered that lining the mould first with muslin stopped sticking and cracking. Now I often keep the pot unscraped, leaving the cloth's texture, or I manipulate a soft-slabbed sand picture into a folded form within the cloth (*see* page 77).

EXPERIMENT

Try the above methods using coloured trailed slips, possibly mixing a little silver-sand into the slip.

First stretch a damp piece of butter-muslin tightly over a dampened batt, tucking the ends underneath. Trail your design onto the cloth, and when the slip has dried, generously brush or pour a coloured backing-slip to cover the picture. (You could also add silver-sand to the backing slip.)

Once this has dried, lay a blanket of fairly damp clay over the backing-slip and roll this on with a rolling-pin. Lift the whole blanket with the cloth-ends that were tucked under your bat, and place it into a mould, smoothing it into position using the cloth-ends, pestling if you want your pattern to spread. Alternatively, flip the blanket over a hump mould. Keep the cloth attached and rub the blanket into place through it. You may want to compress the pattern further by pressing on the blanket with a rubber kidney. After the pot has dried to leather-hard, lift it by the muslin, which can then be gently peeled away – and there is your pattern smoothly inlaid. You can smarten the rim, and possibly burnish the design a little with a spoon.

COLOURED HEXAGONS

Going a stage further, I decided to make a bowl without a backing by just using coloured clay. Marshalling all 24 colours of stoneware clay that I had dyed with oxides, I

Coloured hexagon egg, Jane Waller. Formed from small coloured balls of stoneware clay,
pestled into a two-piece mould and fired using a matt transparent glaze. 25 × 17½ cm (10 × 7 in.)

rolled them into hundreds of balls – slightly smaller than a marble. These I built, line after line, inside a mould, placing each ball next to – as well as above and below – one of a different colour.

I made two discoveries. One was a bore: I needed to make three times as many balls as I thought. The second was a joy: when I took my muslin-covered pestle and, starting from the base, beat the coloured balls to join up one with another, instead of remaining circular, a series of beautiful hexagons appeared (*see* page 79).

GEOMETRIC PATTERNS

I used an extension of the above method to construct a pot from stained stoneware diamonds; then I built one like a brick wall. This had a thin coil wrapped around each rectangle that came out looking like pointing between brick-work (*see* right).

I either gave these pots a matt transparent stoneware glaze, or left them unglazed, firing to the clay's maturing point of 1260–1280°C (2300–2336°F) when the pots became impervious and the colours acquired a slight sheen. While the vessels were still warm from the kiln, I polished them with beeswax, which mellowed the surface and warmed the colours.

MILLEFIORI

While I was lucky enough to do some glass-blowing at the Royal College of Art, London,

Brick wall pot, Jane Waller. Made from rectangles of coloured stoneware, with grouting of coloured clay between and fired unglazed to 1280°C (1976°F) 20 × 10 cm (8 × 4 in.)

39 Happiness bowl, Jane Waller. Strap-rimmed millefiori bowl.
35 × 35 cm (14 × 14 in.). (Courtesy of David and Lyn Griffin)

I learned about making millefiori glass bowls. Rods of coloured glass are fused together then stretched – simply by two people walking speedily away from one another – drawing out the coil between them on a blow-pipe and punty to the desired length. Then the cooled coil is cut through at right-angles to produce minute discs of patterned section, like Brighton rock. These discs are placed in a mould and fused together to make the beautiful millefiori bowls. I picked up individual millefiori pieces like these from the marvering bench and blew them into my glass goblets, so that the pattern enlarged again as the glass wall expanded. I thought this method might be good translated to clay. My pestling would expand the patterned sections inside a plaster mould. Thus began the millefiori clay bowls.

Sections can either be rolled as coils to whatever scale is needed before being cut through; or made from complex blocks of different-coloured shapes, laminated well together, then cut through with either a wire harp or sharp scalpel before making a pattern in the mould.

I like to push the method, using as many as four different types of clay together. Then I increase the molochite content to 15 per cent, which narrows the shrinkage rate, allowing different clays to be used together, as well as reconciling two oxided clays that might otherwise crack when placed side by side. Molochite seems to have a stabilizing effect on oxides.

COLOURS

Wanting more variety of colour, and finding that many pigments burned out at the high stoneware temperatures, I changed to using white earthenware. With my 'setting-up' grant from the Crafts Council, I purchased a large electric glaze-mixer so that I could mix my own coloured clays, using all the ingredients dry. The proportions I use are 1 kg (2 lb 3 oz) of powdered white earthenware to 150 gm (5 oz) of molochite, and earth oxides of up to 5 per cent of one colour.

My colour range has now increased to three dozen samples, and the shades were based on Egyptian frescoes and wooden gessoed mummies' coffins; Pompeii and Herculaneum wall-paintings; Ghirlandaio's frescoes; kelim carpets; and kaleidoscope patterns. The 'greying down' or fresco-powderiness of the colours is obtained by mixing in zinc oxide or minute portions of black iron oxide, nickel, or black body stain – the only commercial stain I use.

Mixing colours is tedious and takes days. With each batch – usually about 2 kg (4 lb 6 oz) – I first add the oxides to a bucket half-filled with water, then the molochite, and lastly the clay, mixing between each addition. Every available mould in the studio is requisitioned, filled with each colour as it is made. These are left until enough water has evaporated for me to form the contents into a pat and wrap it in labelled polythene, then a labelled carrier bag. Finally I put it into a large plastic dustbin. I never wedge the clay as this destroys the kind of tonal differences that I admire in, for example, home-dyed wools. The longer the clay 'rests' before use, the more plastic it is to work. Preparing the clays simultaneously ensures the whole batch has rested for the same amount of time. It is easy at this stage to make test-tiles for any new colours.

METHOD

Before I discovered butter-muslin, the disaster rate for cracking millefiori bowls was upsetting, especially as it had taken ages to form a pattern. If I hammered too hard, the pot stuck to the mould, cracking before I could get it out. If I hammered too softly, the clay millefiori would not join firmly. (I found sump oil, shellac and talc all helped a little before the butter-muslin breakthrough!)

The work is assembled in fairly damp conditions. Millefiori pieces of the same thickness are built up gradually inside the mould. Sometimes pieces are cut as mirror-images of each other, or used in fractal patterns round a bowl. Although I am in charge of the patterning, some distortion is caused by the bashing of the pestle, and revealed only later. I dislike the mindlessness of an agate pattern, though I do use agate pieces within my controlled patterning.

The battering action of the pestle is worked in a spiral from the bottom of the mould whilst the work is rotated on a banding-wheel. Not only does this join the mosaics, it compresses the clay particles tightly to produce a tough wall; also it stretches the clay thinner, and this is when the pattern may move in a mysterious way depending on how or where it is hammered. Soft and hard pieces can be used together at this stage: hard if I want the shape to remain sharp-edged, soft if I want it to spread – but for the latter, obviously, the pestling pressure is decreased or the wall will become too thin.

FINISH

You can form rims by folding the muslin over the edge of the clay and squeezing them to shape. Sometimes great coils of clay are rolled over and these are later strapped with extruded thin ribbon from the indispensible 3 in (7 cm) small clay-extruder, available from most clay stockists (*see* page 94).

When the pot has dried just enough to retain its shape without bending, it is eased from the mould using the excess draped muslin. While the muslin still clings to the pot, I go over the surface, pressing with a hard rubber kidney to join any seams which may not have done so. Back in the mould the pot goes until it has dried to just before leather-hard.

At this stage, I first scrape the inner surface with a metal kidney while the pot is still in the mould so that its support is used to the last. Then I lift it out and peel away the muslin, scraping down the outer wall. The clay is still being compressed at this stage, so that the finished, fired pots are incredibly strong. I always compare this millefiori

Three small millefiori bowls, Jane Waller. Left-hand bowl, $12\frac{1}{2} \times 9$ cm ($5 \times 3\frac{3}{4}$ in.) courtesy of Jennifer Vaughan Rees;
right-hand bowl $11\frac{1}{2} \times 8$ cm ($4\frac{1}{2} \times 3\frac{1}{2}$ in.) *(courtesy of C.A. Waller). (Photo: Frank Thurston)*

Laminated vessel, Dorothy Feibleman. Made of her low-fired translucent (Parian) clay, with design cut and re-cut with a jig, and expanded bands overloaded with copper. (Photo: Thomas Ward; courtesy of Bonhams)

method with the construction of the cranium, for the interlocking pieces of clay, like those of a skull, are knitted together, making the whole tougher than it would be if made from one bone-covering or one sheet of clay.

FIRING

Because the pots may be composed of different clays, I let them dry slowly over a week or two back inside the mould, covered in muslin, with polythene put over the surface. Then later they stay inside loose polythene for a week. Finally uncovered and completely dry, they are bisqued to 1120°C (2048°F).

A matt lead bisilicate glaze (page 92) is applied by the dipping method. I find this infinitely superior to spraying – which I am obliged to use on very large pots – because it fills in any tiny cracks that might appear during bisque-firing. It also gives an even coating of glaze to the different clays, since each clay absorbs only the amount of glaze it requires, whereas spraying tends to overload the white earthenware, whilst starving grogged clays or buff/molochite mixes.

Glaze-firing is to 1080–1100°C (1976–2012°F) cooling slowly to 900°C (1652°F), as crystals will be forming in the glaze over this period. This matt, semi-transparent glaze will have a lovely satin finish – once the correct whiting content (5–10 per cent) has been determined. The colours show through with a softened clarity, which gives surface depth.

SEDIMENTARY MILLEFIORI

It seemed a shame to throw away the coloured clay scrapings from the millefiori pots. Re-used, however, the colour always came out sludge grey because I added water to them in a plastic bowl. Then I found that if I laid a piece of butter-muslin into one of my plaster moulds, filled the mould with the layers of scrapings as they were made, then poured water gently onto these without disturbing the layers, the water was absorbed by the mould while the scrapings remained as individual specks of colour. Later, I lifted the whole lot from the mould still inside its cloth and pressed it gently under a weight – like making cream cheese. When this block was leather-hard, I cut new millefiori, producing agglomerate pieces for new designs. These have that same tufa-light texture as the oolitic bowls (page 55) and absorb a lot of glaze when dipped, but they are immensely strong.

LAMINATION

Dorothy Feibleman makes her ceramics using coloured porcelain in a lamination process, though the pattern goes right through the clay walls since the 'backing' clay is scraped clean away. Her coloured patterns are designed on a rolled-out blanket of porcelain that has been laid in the mould. She uses porcelain slip to make these adhere as well as acting as a cement-like grouting between each piece. Once the pot has dried, it is released from the mould; Dorothy then scrapes away the porcelain blanket from the outside to reveal the pattern beneath. Next she scrapes the inside and neatens the rim. When bone dry, the surface is rubbed down with first a coarse, then smooth wire wool. Very fine, delicate but neatly-patterned bowls are the result (*see* opposite).

CHAPTER TWELVE

COLOUR LAYERING IN THE CLAY BODY

ADDING REFRACTORIES

A refractory is a substance that is resilient to heat, which you can add to the working clay along with other textured materials. Ground shells, powdered potsherds and sands have been used since ancient times. Dust from bricks comes in wonderful colours and makes good dust grog; fire-bricks make fine yellows and beiges. These materials can either be wedged into the clay or inlaid by rolling into slabs before making a pot. (Always wear a mask.)

Refractories added to the pot give a quality to the material that makes it more like a cement to work with, for the clay becomes more tactile and open-bodied. This allows vigorous handling – a textural freedom combined with that of colour and form. The form seems to emanate from the substance, for as well as giving more surface-play, many of the additions will strengthen the pot so that you can increase the variations of thickness more safely, or bend the walls sculpturally into interesting positions.

On irregular pots especially, you can bash

40 Glass pâte de verre vase with intrusions layered into body, Diana Hobson

or roll different materials into the surface before this becomes too hard. Press crushed glass into the surface; add sand and grog coloured with oxides; or combine ground-up bisqued pieces of coloured ceramic. Make your own coloured grog by using raw clay first coloured with oxide, then dried and pestled in a mortar to the consistency required. Now fire this inside an unglazed pot and use it to speckle your pots. Mica chips and some natural oxides like ilmenite, iron spangles or manganese will add further specklings.

All these additions allow you to be far more inventive with ceramics. Forms acquire a gutsy, sculptural strength, which can aspire to the monumental. Later, grogged areas can be scraped to expose a scratched, mottled surface, or burnished and pressed further into the pot's walls.

Diana Hobson, working in glass, has been experimenting with inclusions in her beautiful pâte de verre vases. She lodges pieces of brick-dust, metal, etc. within the surface of her mould-wall where they become fused with the glass paste when this is fired inside

*Pot, Sarah Radstone, 1988. 60 cm (23½ in.).
(Photo: George Meyrick)*

*Leaning and thrusting series, Ewen
Henderson, 1988. Bone china and porcelain
mix, laminated onto stoneware, 61 cm (2 ft)*

her special moulds. Although created in a
different medium, her work should inspire
many potters.

Many modern potters roll clay containing
refractory materials into coils and then flatten
them into slabs. Often these are cut into pre-
formed curves – like pieces of dress pattern.
Sarah Radstone, for example, builds her
sensitive constructions from leather-hard
slabbed pieces making a kind of tailored
assymetry. She used a modern imagery of
random wall-markings, scratched paints,
worn surfaces, etc. inspired by the
surroundings of her Brixton studio.

Ewen Henderson laminates his onto a
central core of Crank or stoneware to prevent
splitting – although this itself can be an
attractive feature. He then incorporates glaze
materials, adding silicon carbide and glaze
stains into the clay with opacifiers such as
zinc oxide and titanium dioxide and adds
additional glaze to the surface, designed to
reveal the colours in the clay. His glace recipe
is as follows:

Whiting 100	Soda feldspar 100
Lithium carbonate 10	Tin oxide 10
China clay 70	Vanadium pentoxide 10

His pieces are fired to 1260C (2300°F), in an
electric kiln. (If you are adding additional
glaze as well as refractories, take care to raise
the pots on old, bat-washed pieces of kiln-
shelf so that kiln-shelves are not spoiled. Also
fire the pots separately in case they explode.)

RAKU

Raku is an exciting method with which to experiment when colouring the clay body. With its accelerated ageing process, the firing adds pattern-layers of its own whilst drawing out the colours you have stained, changing them into 'something rich and strange'.

I use the pinching method for raku as I can have maximum handling throughout the process. A grogged clay like 'T' Material is excellent to choose, since being white it needs only small amounts of stain to obtain good colour. Walls of varying thickness will also survive the firing. Ungrogged stained stoneware can be used successfully for raku, provided that the forms are small and enclosed. The inclusion of 10 to 15 per cent molochite strengthens the body, and gently speckles the surface. I use a combination of 'T' Material and buff stoneware, well-mixed with the stain. The stoneware gives warmth to the finished raku, softening the colours, whilst giving a less rough texture for scraping down.

I use small quantities of mixed oxides to obtain shades similar to those in the millefiori method, often 'greying down' a strong oxide with iron chromate. Try tiny amounts of the coppers and cobalts together; different

Treasure chest, Jane Waller, 1987. Millefiori pieces and coloured slip inlaid into heavily-grogged earthenware, then glazed with earthenware glaze (p. 80). 60 × 50 cm (24 × 20 in.)

proportions will produce unlimited shades of bluey-greens or greeny-blues. Smaller amounts of chrome added to these, will convert them to peacocks or turquoise. Small quantities of red iron oxide will give pink; manganese dioxide and cobalt carbonate, bluish-mauve.

I mix the colours into damp clay by making a hole in the centre of a wedged ball of clay, adding the stains – and molochite if the body is ungrogged – and mixing this to a paste with the surrounding clay. Mixing the clay wet means that however thoroughly the colour is wedged, it happily is never mixed completely, and so gives tone changes in the finished pot. (Continue working as with the pinching method described in chapter 4.)

I often divide the clay, using one part to form the base and side walls – usually up to where there is to be a change in silhouette or to where the pot's widest point will be. I may add some millefiori pieces – not haphazardly, but where they will complement the form. However, adding millefiori pieces early on, helps to direct the shape of the piece, as the millefiori creates new wall-width or 'tucks' of extra material that can be pinched out. Make sure that any millefiori additions have the same dampness as the mother clay they join.

The second portion of clay is now used to

Ridged pinch pot, Jane Waller, 1987. 'T' Material, buff stoneware and molochite mix, stained with oxides and rakued. 14 × 10 cm (5½ × 4 in.). (Photo: Frank Thurston)

complete the pot. You can add this in strips, pinching into clay spirals or funnel-shapes. Sometimes appliqué pieces are added to the surface in plain or stained 'T' Material. If these motifs are slightly wetter than the parent body, you can press them into the surface slightly with your thumb, and support the inside with your finger. Alternatively, tap them smartly with a wooden baton, while supporting the inside, inlaying them with a well-defined edge. If the appliqué pieces are drier than the pot, they will hardly change shape when tapped, remaining embossed on the surface (*see* back cover). Often I encourage star motifs to curl over the rim, adding irregularities. The pot is scraped when leather-hard until the form is taut. Pots are bisque-fired for safety instead of fired 'green'.

To reveal the colours inside the clay body during the firing, I use a transparent high alkaline frit raku glaze, as itemized below:

85% Potterycraft high alkaline frit P.2962
15% Ball clay
2% Glaze suspender

Even at the glazing stage new surface layers can be created. Where areas are left unglazed, these will stay matt black. And where the glaze collects naturally in areas, an increased opacity will dull the colours, softening their emergence through the glaze. (The inside must be glazed, however, if it is to be used as a container, as rakued pots are porous and soft.) Dry the pots thoroughly before placing them in the kiln.

FIRING

A raku firing is best done using an outdoor kiln where excess smoke and flames will be less of a hazard. At first the kiln is brought up slowly, then quickly to reach between 900°C (1652°F) and 1000°C degrees (1832°F), or when the surface of the pots is molten and evenly-glowing. Now the kiln is quickly opened, a pot grasped with the tongs and carried from the kiln to be bedded down in a bin of sawdust. Further sawdust is hastily put over the top, and the lid is replaced.

REDUCTION

Now comes the time when the elements take charge. Under the sawdust coating the combusting material, deprived of oxygen, seeks to draw it from the oxides within the clay body. In the process, stains that have been put inside the clay-body or on the surface, are altered, causing rainbow iridescence or, if in a subdued mood, warm-coloured tones will be drawn from the stains without any razzmatazz. 2 per cent ferric oxide, for example, will with 0.5 per cent of copper, produce yellow. But 3–6 per cent of copper oxide, when deprived of oxygen, will often flash to shades of red, or reveal metallic colour in areas of its own serendipitous choosing. When small amounts of cobalt and copper or nickel are added together, a silvery metallic lustre sometimes results. The sooner the pot is placed inside the sawdust the greater the chance of lustre effects occurring – but you never know what the effect will be.

Meanwhile, on the unglazed surface, which is porous and soft owing to the low firing of the material, the burning sawdust will deposit its free carbon to mark the pot-surface from shades of grey right through to a deep carbonaceous black, making areas that contrast glazed and unglazed. If this happens at the bottom of the pot, it will impart a shadowed area, which helps to raise the pot's silhouette above its base.

CRAZING

The final stage of decoration is revealed when the pot is excavated from the burnt sawdust (usually after five to twenty minutes), and plunged into a bucket of water. The surface is discovered to be covered with crazing. The water, as well as preventing the colours from re-oxidizing in the air, sets the reduction patterning picked out by carbon deposited in the interstices of the crazing.

Crazing alters according to the nature of the surface. Flat areas attract large-scale crazing, while over prominences and around curves runs a fine close network. Pitting and spots break through the glaze from beneath and soften the effect of the glaze whilst adding surface depth. This depth can be further emphasized by your dipping the finished pot, when still warm, into a gentle stain dissolved in water, or some diluted ink and allowing it to fill the crazing. Wipe off the excess to leave a delicate vein of cobwebbing.

CHAPTER THIRTEEN

A FEW GLAZES

Glaze is but the glass of a pair of spectacles through which one looks into the clay

Kenzan, 1737

EARTHENWARE

FIRING TEMPERATURES ARE 1000°–1100°C (1832–2012°F)

Industrial earthenware glaze forms a hard skin covering the pot instead of fusing with the body – which is what usually happens at stoneware temperatures. Often this gives a glass-like quality which I find distressing. An unsympathetic shiny glaze can easily spoil colour-work beneath, producing the same harshness as a door coated with crude gloss varnish. Light is bounced brightly from the surface rather than absorbed. Students often wet coloured bisque-fired pottery with the tongue or put it under a running tap and say, '*I wish it would stay like that – smooth and matt but with the colour glowing through*' and I tend to agree. I need to work at low temperatures in order to keep the soft, mid-tone colours I like; fired at higher stoneware temperatures, many such colours would burn away or darken considerably, giving a narrower tonal range. Yet, like many others, I still like the idea of some of my pottery being functional – impervious, washable, hygienic – which is partly what a glaze is for.

HERE ARE NINE WAYS TO GET THE 'TONGUE-WETTED' LOOK:

1 Fire to a low bisque (800–900°C (1472–1652°F)), then sand-paper with fine 'wet and dry' carborundum paper until the surface is smooth. Now refire to the clay's maturing point in the second firing, without a glaze. (The maturing temperature is the point at which you get maximum strength with minimum distortion.) This process is good for stained porcelains, too. If stoneware is treated in this way, the silica in the body forms a slight self-glazing. The surface can be polished with beeswax while it is still warm from the kiln.

2 Put the glaze on, then wipe it off with a damp sponge, leaving only a very fine layer which will go semi-matt when fired. This surface can be waxed as above.

3 Use a matt transparent glaze like that I use over my millefiori. It is velvety but still brings out the colour, softening the light by absorbing it.

4 Glaze the pot, thus water-proofing it, then, after firing, sand-blast the top surface. This 'ages' the surface, breaking it down into either a pitted or smooth silkiness, depending on what coarseness of sand is used. (This, if you are lucky enough to have access to a sand-blaster.)

5 Fire an unglazed slip-covered or engobed body to its vitrification point, (see Elizabeth Fritsch's work page 67).

6 Sawdust fire burnished, bisqued or slip-covered work (page 64).

7 Reduce the ceramic form using the tin-foil method (page 64).

8 Use the soft, crazed surface of a rakued glaze (page 90).

9 Use a crackle glaze. One of the most beautiful is a soft white unifying tin glaze which looks particularly nice on a pinch pot. I have experimented with several crackle glazes where the crackle-size alters.

Here are some glazes to try:

WHITE CRACKLE GLAZE (JANE WALLER) 1050°C (1922°F)

The glaze should be used on an open-bodied clay. Use a buff/'T' Material mix, and glaze 10 to 15 degrees *below* the bisqued temperature.

Borax frit 70	Whiting 5
Nepheline syenite 25	China clay 10
Tin oxide 4	

MATT MILLEFIORI TRANSPARENT GLAZE (JANE WALLER) 1060–1080°C (1940–1976°F)

Lead bisilicate 64	Cornish stone 9.4
China clay 21	Whiting 5

This is good used over stained white earthenware and slipware.

MATT SATIN GLAZE (BILL HALL) 1060–1080°C (1940–1976°F)

Lead sesquisilicate 55	Whiting 10
Potash feldspar 25	China clay 30

Add 3 per cent barium carbonate for a smoother surface.
Add 5 per cent tin oxide or zinc oxide for cream.
Add 2 per cent copper oxide and 6 per cent red iron oxide for matt black.

The four nicest shiny earthenware glazes I know are:

BLACK SILVERY SHINY GLAZE (JANE WALLER) 1060°C (1940°F)

Podmore's 2105 clear earthenware glaze, 100 copper oxide 10

This is good over white slip.

TRANSPARENT SHINY GLAZE (TONY BIRKS) 1060°C (1940°F)

Lead bisilicate 56	China clay 7
Potash feldspar 30	Whiting 5

Add 10 per cent tin oxide for an opaque white majolica.

LUSH GREENY-TURQUOISE GLAZE (VANESSA WALLER) 1080°C (1976°F)

Potash feldspar 18	Borax frit 34
Flint 23	Whiting 9
China clay 3	Zinc oxide 9
Copper oxide 3	Cobalt oxide 1

Greeny when thin; turquoise when thickly applied.

STONEWARE

Stoneware pots are usually fired 1240–1280°C (2264–2336°F) so that the clay particles fuse in a homogenous mass and react with the glaze, which becomes part of the pot itself. As the name implies, this gives a stone-like quality: strong, dense and non-porous. This durability means that stoneware can be used for cooking and eating from. Magnesium and some nepheline syenite glazes have a pitted matt quality. Nepheline syenite will, when mixed with oxides in a creamy glaze, produce specklings and a profusion of colour-tones, especially if applied over a white slip. Glaze will run darker or more opaque where it pools in hollows or runs off edges, accentuating form.

A single glaze will give a pot classic poise. The pot is seen as a whole and the form will combine with whichever smooth or textured quality is chosen. Give the pot an overlapping of two glazes or two of one, and a new pattern and third colour is created where they combine.

As a general rule, a dipped pot should dry in seven seconds. If less, it is too thinly glazed; if more, too much, and the glaze needs diluting.

SMOOTH OPAQUE (RHODES) 1260°C (2300°F)

Good over slips or with oxides on top. Milky when thickly applied. Nice over porcelain with copper oxide or copper carbonate beneath.

Potash feldspar 49   China clay 25
Dolomite 22   Whiting 4

STONEWARE CRACKLE GLAZE (K. CLARK) 1275°C (2327°F)

Soda feldspar 80   China clay 10
Whiting 10

After cooling the surface can be brushed with an oxide or stain to accentuate the crackle, or refired so that the oxide combines with the glaze.

BLUE WITH CREAM HIGHLIGHTS (SIR JOHN CASS COLLEGE) 1260°C (2300°F)

When applied thickly, this becomes green with yellow-brown highlights and speckles. An effective glaze for sculpture. Good for overlapping.

Potash feldspar 33   Dolomite 33
China clay 33   Rutile 2.50
   Cobalt dioxide 0.25

BLACK SPECKLE GREEN (SIR JOHN CASS COLLEGE) 1260°C (2300°F)

Potash feldspar 55   Dolomite 5
Barium carbonate 20   China clay 10
Flint 10   Copper oxide 4
   Tin oxide 6

BLACK/TURQUOISE (SIR JOHN CASS COLLEGE) 1260°C (2300°F)

Potash feldspar 100   Barium carbonate 40
China clay 20   Flint 12
Whiting 20   Copper carbonate 4

PORCELAIN

Porcelain will look and feel as smooth as ivory or dense as a fine, polished sea-shell when fired very high to 1300°C (2372°F) (Bone china to 1240–1260°C (2264–2300°F)). If scraped thin enough, porcelain will fire translucent.

TRANSPARENT CHUN GLAZE (PETER YATES) 1260°C (2300°F)

Feldspar 50   Zinc oxide 6
Flint 23   Whiting 19

MAUVE SPECKLE (SIR JOHN CASS COLLEGE) 1260°C (2300°F)

Potash feldspar 49   Dolomite 23
Whiting 3.50   China clay 25
Copper carbonate 1

Add 0.125 per cent cobalt oxide if blue is required.
  (For further glaze information and recipes, refer to the *Dictionary of Ceramics* or *Clay and Glaze Book* in *Further Reading*.

POSTSCRIPT

Pots and all other artifacts serve the mind as well as the body. They are born of a marriage between use and beauty. They are not just art for art's sake so much as art for life's sake. Whether less or more conscious they are extensions of people striving to make human products with as much wholeness and naturalness as a sea-shell or the wing of a butterfly: if human beings do not make peace with themselves as part of the whole of nature – how can they expect maturity either in themselves or in their pots?

Bernard Leach, *Beyond East and West*, 1962

SUPPLIERS

BRITAIN

Potclays Ltd
Brickiln Lane
Etruria
Stoke-on-Trent
Staffordshire
Tel. 0782 29816

Fulham Pottery
8–10 Ingate Place
London
SW8 3NS
Tel. 01 720 0050

Potterycrafts Ltd
Campbell Road
Stoke-on-Trent
Staffordshire
ST4 4ET
Tel. 0782 272444

and at
75 Silver Street
London N18

29 Wates Way
Willow Tree Industrial Estate
Mitcham
Surrey
CR4 4HR
Tel. 01 648 3356

Deancraft Fahey Ltd
12 Spedding Road
Fenton Industrial Estate
Stoke-on-Trent
Staffordshire
ST4 2ST

Alec Tiranti
Sculptors Tools & Materials
27 Warren Street
London
W1
Tel. 01 636 8565

Clayglaze Ltd.
Talbot Rd,
Richmansworth
Herts. WD3 1HW

AMERICA

Stewert Clay Co Inc
133 Mulberry Street
New York
NY 10013

Jack D Wolfe Co Inc
Brooklyn
NY

Sculpture House Inc
38 East 30 Street
New York
NY 10016

Newton Potter's Supply Inc
96 Rumford Avenue
West Newton
Mass 02165

Duncan Ceramics Products Inc
PO Box 7827
Fresno
California 93727

Bell Ceramics Inc
Box 697 Clermont
Florida 32711

FURTHER READING

BOOKS AND CATALOGUES

Birks, Tony. *Hans Coper*, Collins, 1983

Bourriau, J. *Nile Pottery*, Cambridge University Press, 1981. Catalogue by Janine Bourriau (Exhibition Oct/Dec 1981)

Cameron, Elisabeth and Lewis, Phillipa (Eds). *Potters on Pottery*, Evans Brothers, 1976.

Clark, Kenneth. *The Potter's Manual*, Macdonald, 1983

Cooper, Emmanuel. *Handbook of Pottery*, Longman, 1970

Cooper, Emmanuel. *A History of World Pottery*, Batsford, 1988

Cooper, Emmanuel. *Cooper's Book of Glaze Recipes*, Batsford, 1987

Cooper, Emmanuel and Lewenstein, Eileen (Eds). *New Ceramics*, Studio Vista, 1974.

Feininger, Andreas. *Shells*, Thames and Hudson, 1972

·Fournier, Robert. *Illustrated Dictionary of Practical Pottery*, Van Nostrand Reinhold, 1977

Frank, L.P. *Historic Pottery of the Pueblo Indians*, New York Graphic Society, 1984

Fujioka, Ryoichi. *Shino and Oribe Ceramics*, Japanese Arts Library, 1977

Hamer, Frank. *Dictionary of Ceramics*, Pitman, 1975

Honey, W.B. *The Art of the Modern Potter*, Faber and Faber, 1944

Jenyns, Soame. *Japanese Pottery*, Faber and Faber, 1971

Kidder, Edward. *Prehistoric Japanese Art: Joman Pottery*, Kodanscha International Ltd, 1968

ICA catalogue. *Fast Forward: New Directions in British Ceramics*, March, 1985

Leach, Bernard. *A Potter's Book*, Faber and Faber, 1988

Leach, Bernard. *Kenzan and his tradition*, Faber and Faber, 1966

Leach, Bernard. *Beyond East and West*, Faber and Faber, 1985

Mills, Dick and Ververs, Gwynne. *Practical Encyclopaedia of Freshwater Tropical Aquarium Fishes*, Salamander, 1982

Pictou, J. *African Textiles*, British Museum Publications Ltd, 1979

Morris, Desmond. *The Art of Ancient Cyprus*, Phaidon, 1985

Postma, C. *Plant Life in Miniature*, Harrap, 1960

Prodan, Mario. *The Art of the T'ang Potter*, Thames and Hudson, 1960

Rawson, Philip. *Ceramics*, Oxford University Press, 1971

Rawson, Philip. *Drawing*, University of Pennsylvania Publications, 1983

Rogers, Mary. *On Pottery and Porcelain*, Alphabooks, 1979

Sutherland, Brian. *Glazes from Natural Sources*, Batsford, 1987

MAGAZINES

Cooper, Emmanuel and Lewenstein, Eileen. *Ceramic Review*. Published at: 21 Carnaby Street, London W1V 1PH

INDEX